# CHILDCRAFT
## SCIENCE AND INDUSTRY

# Childcraft

## IN FIFTEEN VOLUMES

•

## VOLUME NINE

## SCIENCE AND INDUSTRY

## FIELD ENTERPRISES EDUCATIONAL CORPORATION
### Merchandise Mart Plaza · Chicago 54, Illinois

# CHILDCRAFT

*Acknowledgment*

Grateful acknowledgment is made to the author of this book, John
Sternig, M.A., Assistant Superintendent of Schools, Glencoe, Ill.

# WHAT IS IN THIS BOOK

LIVING THINGS                                                    PAGE

Living Wonders . . . . . . . . .                                  3

Some Living Things Are Big, Some
   Are Little . . . . . . . .                       6

Some Things Live a Long Time,
   Some a Short Time . . . . . .                     7

Where Do Animals Come From? . . . . .                             8

Where Did You Come From? . . . . .                                9

Are All Living Things Born from Mothers? .                        10

Many Baby Animals Are Weak and Helpless
   When They Are Born . . . . . .                   11

Other Babies Are Not Quite as Helpless . .                       12

Still Other Baby Animals Are Left
   to Take Care of Themselves . . . .               13

Many Baby Animals Learn
   from Their Mothers . . . . .                     14

Boys and Girls Learn Much More than
   Animal Babies Can . . . . .                      15

Some Babies Look Altogether Different
   from Their Parents . . . . .                     16

Frog Babies Look Different, Too . . . .                          18

Some Babies Have Many Grownups to Take
   Care of Them . . . . .                           19

Be Your Own Zoo Keeper . . . . .                                 20

Your Zoo Cage . . . . . .                                        21

Here Are Some Insects You May Find
   for Your Zoo . . . . . .                         22

Where Do Plants Come From? . . . . .                             24

What Happens When You Plant Bean Seeds? .                        25

Do Plants Grow Only from Seeds? . . .                            26

Seeds Which Are Not Really Seeds . . . .                         27

What Do Plants and Animals Need to
   Live and Grow? . . . . .                         28

How Do Living Things Get the Air
   They Need? . . . . .                             29

Where Do Living Things Get the Food
   They Need? . . . . .                             30

All Food Really Comes from Green Plants .                        31

How Do Green Plants Make Their Food? .                           32

How Does Water Get Up into the Leaves? . .                       33

What Happens to the Food a Plant Makes? .                        34

How Do Leaves Grow on Trees? . . . .                             36

Why Do Leaves Turn Color and Drop
   in the Fall? . . . . . .                         37

How Do Animals Protect Themselves? . . .                         38

Color and Shape Help to Protect
   Some Animals . . . . . .                         39

Other Animals Have Weapons to Protect
   Themselves . . . . .                             40

These Animals Fight with Their Feet . . .                        41

These Animals Fight with Their Teeth . .                         42

Some Animals Have Armor . . . . .                                43

Many Animals Use Poison . . . . .                                44

Other Animal Weapons . . . . .                                   45

Do Plants Protect Themselves? . . . .                            46

Where Do Animals Live? . . . . .                                 47

Underground Homes . . . . .                                      48

Don't Bother This Home! . . . . .                                49

Make Your Own Home for Water Animals
   and Plants . . . . . .                           50

Making Your Own Home for Land Animals
   and Plants . . . . .                             52

Which Belongs with Which? . . . . .                              54

The People Who Live in the World . . .                           55

Different Peoples Have Different Homes .                         56

What Kinds of Plants Are There
   in the World? . . . . .                          57

What Kinds of Animals Are There
   in the World? . . . . .                          58

Some Animals Which Have No Backbones .                           58

Animals with Jointed Legs . . . . .                              59

Animals Which Have Backbones . . . .                             60

Animals Which Give Milk to Their Babies .                        61

Some Plants and Animals Are too Small
   to be Seen! . . . . .                            62

Let's Try an Experiment! . . . . .                               63

Plants and Animals Depend on Each Other .                        64

How Plants and Animals Help Us . . . .                           65

## THE EARTH WE LIVE ON

PAGE

| | |
|---|---|
| What the Earth Is Like | 68 |
| High Lands of the Earth | 69 |
| The Lowlands | 70 |
| Rivers, Valleys, and Canyons | 71 |
| The Hot and Wet Lands | 72 |
| Hot and Dry Lands | 73 |
| The Cold Lands | 74 |
| Oceans, Lakes, and Swamps | 75 |
| How Do We Know the Earth Is Round? | 76 |
| What Makes Day and Night? | 78 |
| Make Your Own Day and Night | 79 |
| The Earth Travels Around the Sun, Too | 80 |
| Why Do We Have Spring, Summer, Fall, and Winter? | 81 |
| What Keeps the Earth Moving Around the Sun? | 82 |
| What Makes Things Fall to the Earth? | 83 |
| What Do You Mean When You Say "Up" or "Down"? | 84 |
| How to Find North During the Day | 85 |
| Where Are South, East, and West? | 86 |
| How Can We Find North at Night? | 87 |
| What Else Do We Use to Find Our Way? | 88 |
| How to Use a Road Map | 89 |
| How Do Sailors and Airmen Find Their Way? | 90 |
| The Earth Is Surrounded by a Blanket of Air | 91 |
| How Do We Know Air Is Real? | 92 |
| Air Has Weight, Too | 93 |
| Air Works for Us | 94 |
| Fun with Air | 95 |
| Air on the Move | 96 |
| What Makes Air Move? | 97 |
| What Makes Our Weather? | 98 |
| How Does Water Get into the Air? | 99 |
| Cloud Shapes in the Sky | 100 |
| What Makes It Rain? | 101 |
| Make Your Own Rain | 102 |
| Snow | 103 |
| Hail and Sleet | 104 |

PAGE

| | |
|---|---|
| Make Your Own Dew and Frost | 105 |
| What Makes Thunder and Lightning? | 106 |
| What Does the Weatherman Do? | 108 |
| How You Can Tell How Hot or How Cold It Is | 109 |
| Keep Your Own Weather Records | 110 |
| A Weather Calendar | 111 |
| What Happens to the Rain After It Falls? | 112 |
| Where Does the Water We Use Come From? | 113 |
| Water Works for Us | 114 |
| What Is the Earth Made of? | 115 |
| A Mountain That Breathes Fire and Smoke | 116 |
| A Giant Water Pistol | 117 |
| Water Changes the Surface of the Earth | 118 |
| Wind and Ice Change the Earth's Surface | 119 |
| Man, too, Has Changed the Earth's Surface | 120 |
| How Soil Is Made | 121 |
| You Can Make Your Own Soil | 121 |
| How Soil Works for Us | 122 |
| How Do We Use Sand and Clay? | 123 |
| What Are Rocks Good For? | 124 |
| Collecting Stones | 125 |
| What We Get from the Earth | 126 |
| More Minerals We Get from the Earth | 128 |
| What the Earth We Live on Means to Us | 130 |

## THE SKY ABOVE US

| | |
|---|---|
| What Can You See in the Daytime Sky? | 133 |
| What Can You See in the Sky at Night? | 134 |
| How High Is the Sky? | 135 |
| What Makes the Sky Blue? | 136 |
| The Brightest Object in the Sky | 137 |
| How Big Is the Sun? How Far Away Is It? | 138 |
| What Makes a Rainbow? | 139 |
| Make Your Own Rainbow | 140 |
| Clouds in the Sky | 141 |
| These Clouds Bring Rain | 142 |
| Clouds That Look Like Sheets | 143 |
| Do Stars Really Twinkle? | 144 |
| Why Do the Stars Look so Small? | 145 |

PAGE

How to Make a Five-Pointed Star with One Snip of the Scissors . . . . . 146

Star Pictures in the Sky . . . . . . . 147

The Big Dipper . . . . . . . . 148

Star Pictures and Their Stories . . . . . 149

Orion, the Mighty Hunter . . . . . . 150

The Scorpion . . . . . . . . . 151

Leo, the Lion . . . . . . . . 152

How Many Stars Can You See in the Sky? . 153

How Many Stars Are There? . . . . . 154

Traveling by the Stars . . . . . . 155

Where Do the Stars Go in the Daytime? . . 156

Do Some Stars Have Tails? . . . . . 157

What Are Shooting Stars? . . . . . . 158

Meteors Which Hit the Earth . . . . . 159

The Moon Is Our Nearest Sky Neighbor . 160

Many Moons Ago . . . . . . . 161

Is There a Man in the Moon? . . . . 162

What Is the Moon Really Like? . . . . 163

The Changing Moon . . . . . . 164

Why Does the Moon Seem to Change Its Shape? . . . . . . . . . 166

Nine Sky Wanderers . . . . . . 167

The Planets Are All Different . . . . 168

What Else Do We Find in the Sky? . . . 169

Studying the Sky Through the "Big Eye" . 170

Who Will Be the First Space Man? . . . 172

Traveling in Space . . . . . . . 173

How Fast Will Space Ships Have to Travel? . . . . . . . . . 174

## The Machines We Use

Machines in the Home . . . . . . 177

Digging Machines . . . . . . . 178

Building Machines . . . . . . . 179

Some Hand Tools Are Building Machines, Too . . . . . . . 180

Machines on the Farm . . . . . . 181

Machines That Go Places . . . . . 182

A Machine That Flies . . . . . . 183

How to Make a Paper Airplane That Will Fly . . . . . . . . 184

PAGE

A Machine That Goes Under the Water . . 185

Machines to Play With . . . . . . 186

Which Is Easier? . . . . . . . 187

Which Is Faster? . . . . . . . 188

The Wheel, One of Man's Greatest Inventions . . . . . . . . 189

Making a Wheel Toy from a Spool . . . 190

Wheels Need Axles Before They Will Work . 191

Wheels That Turn But Go Nowhere . . . 192

Wheels with Teeth . . . . . . 193

Pulling with Pulleys . . . . . . 194

Fun with Pulleys . . . . . . 195

How to Lift a Big Weight with One Finger . . . . . . . . 196

How a Lever Works Best . . . . . 197

How We Use Levers . . . . . . 198

More Levers . . . . . . . . 199

Hill Machines . . . . . . . . 200

How We Use Hill Machines . . . . 201

Fun with a Homemade Hill Machine . . . 202

Screws Are Machines, Too . . . . . 203

Machines with Sharp Edges and Points . 204

Several Machines in One . . . . . 205

Machines Will Not Work by Themselves . . 206

Animal Muscles Make Some Machines Work . 207

We Use Our Own Muscles to Make Other Machines Work . . . . . 208

Air Works for Us in Some Machines . . . 209

We Use Air Under Pressure in Other Machines . . . . . . . 210

Machines Run by Liquids . . . . . 211

How to Make a Water Wheel . . . . 212

Heat Runs Many of Our Machines . . . 213

Electricity Works for Us, Too . . . . 214

Where Does Electricity Come From? . . . 215

How Does Electricity Get to Our Homes? . . 216

How to Make Electricity Move Things . . 217

Putting Magnets to Work . . . . . 218

How Electricity Heats Things . . . . 219

Electricity Can Be Changed into Light . . 220

Where Else Does Light Come From? . . . 221

Putting Light to Work . . . . . . 222

                                          PAGE
What Is Sound? . . . . . . . .    223
How Sound Works for Us . . . . .   224

## How Science and Industry Help Us

Where Do They Come From? . . . . .   227
The Foods We Eat . . . . . . .    228
Where Does Our Food Come From? . . .   229
Some of Our Food Comes from the Water . .   230
Foods from Faraway Places . . . . .   231
What Happens to the Food That Is
    Grown on the Farm? . . . . . .   232
How Are Foods Kept from Spoiling? . . .   233
Keeping Fresh Foods Fresh . . . . .   234
The Foods You Should Eat . . . . .   235
The Clothes We Wear . . . . . .   236
Woolen Clothes to Keep You Warm . . .   237
Cotton Clothes to Keep You Cool . . .   238
You, too, Can Weave . . . . . .   239
Silk for Dressing Up . . . . . .   240
Clothes Made from Wood, Coal, and Milk . .   241
Clothes Made from Leather . . . . .   242
The Shoes We Wear . . . . . .   243
The Houses We Live In . . . . . .   244
What Is a House Made of? . . . . .   245
Many Houses Are Made of Wood . . .   246
Other Houses Are Made of Brick and Stone .   248
Houses Built of Man-Made Stone . . .   249
Other Things Made of Concrete . . . .   250
Iron and Steel for Buildings . . . . .   251
Glass for Our Windows . . . . . .   252
Other Objects Made of Glass . . . .   253
Pots, Pans, and Dishes . . . . . .   254

                                          PAGE
Other Objects Made of Clay . . . . .   255
How a House Is Built . . . . . .   256
How Houses Are Heated . . . . .   258
How We Travel . . . . . . .   259
Cars, Buses, and Trucks . . . . .   260
What Makes a Car Go? . . . . . .   261
Where Does the Gasoline Come From? . .   262
Rubber Tires to Ride on . . . . .   263
We Fly Through the Air . . . . .   264
Over the Rails We Go! . . . . . .   265
Over Bridges and Under Mountains
    and Rivers . . . . . . .   266
Across Rivers, Lakes, and Oceans . . .   267
Coal for Steam and Heat . . . . .   269
How We Share What We Know . . . .   270
Where Does Your Telephone Reach? . . .   271
How to Use the Telephone . . . . .   272
Listening to Radio . . . . . .   274
Looking at Television . . . . . .   275
Books to Read and Enjoy . . . . .   276
Books for Everything . . . . . .   277
Where Books Are Kept . . . . . .   278
Reading the Newspaper . . . . . .   279
Learning from Pictures . . . . . .   280
The Paper We Use . . . . . . .   282
Some Things for Which Paper Is Used . . .   283
Other Ways in Which Science and
    Industry Help Us . . . . . .   284
Helping Our Policemen to Help Us . . .   285
Helping to Keep Us Well . . . . .   286
Making It Easier for Us to Learn . . .   287
Looking Ahead . . . . . . .   288

# LIVING THINGS

H. Armstrong Roberts

ALL LIVING THINGS are either plants or animals. There are many, many different kinds of each. All are alike in some ways and different in others.

Where do these living things come from? How do they grow and change? What do they need to keep alive?

How do living things get their food? How do they protect themselves? What kinds of homes do animals make? Which plants and animals are useful to man? Which are harmful? How do we depend on plants and animals?

Answers to these and to many other questions will be found in these pages. There will be many interesting things for you to do. And, as you study these animals and plants, you will never cease to wonder about the living things around you.

## Living Wonders

Living things are among the most interesting wonders of nature. That is one reason why you enjoy going to the circus, to the zoo, and to the farm. Almost everywhere you go, you will find living things of one kind or another.

It may be a cuddly kitten

. . . or
a galloping
horse.

It may be
a slow-moving snail

. . . a noisy bluejay

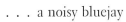

Spencer: American Museum of Natural History; Jenkins; Lambert

. . . a busy bee

. . . a graceful tulip

. . . a crawling worm

. . . a lovely sunflower

. . . a perky chipmunk

. . . a playful dog

. . . a land turtle

Spencer; Lambert; Ewing Galloway

. . . a clucking hen

. . . or
a fuzzy-headed
dandelion.

5

## Some Living Things Are Big, Some Are Little

Some living things are big, like this hippopotamus.

Other living things are small, like this violet and this ladybug.

Still others are so small that you cannot even see them without a micro-scope.

Lambert; Spencer; Hillman

# Some Things Live a Long Time, Some a Short Time

Some living things, like these giant redwood trees, live for thousands of years.

Others, like this grasshopper and butterfly, live for only a few months after they have grown up.

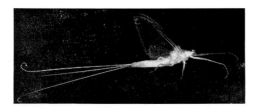

Still others, like this mayfly, live only a few days.

Where do all these living things come from? Let's find out!

### Where Do Animals Come From?

Where did these little pigs come from?

Where did the kittens come from?

Do you know where this calf came from?

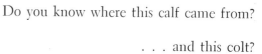

. . . and this colt?

H. Armstrong Roberts; Wallace, Black Star;
J. C. Allen and Son; Ewing Galloway

Each animal on this page was born from a mother. It had a father, too.

8

## Where Did You Come From?

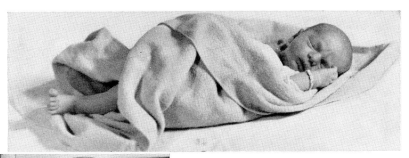

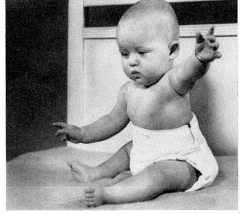

You were born from your mother, too. At first you were small and helpless. You could not talk, you could not walk, and you could not feed or dress yourself. Your father and mother had to do everything for you.

Later on, you learned to sit up

. . . to crawl

. . . and to walk and run.

Tana Hoban, Rapho-Guillumette;
Garrison, Black Star; Lambert

Boys and girls take many years to grow up. That is why your father and mother take care of you. They give you the food, the shelter, the clothing, and the love that you need.

## Are All Living Things Born from Mothers?

Birds are born from eggs laid by the mother bird.

Spiders, insects, and some other animals are also born from eggs.

Trees grow from seeds which have been made by parent trees.

Lambert; Spencer

Ferns come from seedlike spores made by the parent plant.

Living things come from parents that are like them. But not all are born from parents in the same way.

## Many Baby Animals
## Are Weak and Helpless
## When They Are Born

When puppies are born, they cannot even see. Their eyes are closed for about ten days. The mother dog has to take care of them. For six weeks, the puppies eat no other food except the milk they get from their mother.

Ylla, Rapho-Guillumette

Baby rabbits have their eyes closed for ten or twelve days after they are born. They do not even have any fur on their bodies when they are born.

Baby kittens cannot see for eight or ten days after they are born. The mother cat takes care of them and feeds them while they are helpless.

What other animals can you think of that have to be cared for by their mothers?

11

The chick keeps pecking and pushing at the shell. The tiny hole becomes a wide crack and the shell breaks open.

When a baby chick is ready to come out of the egg, it pecks a hole in the shell.

Then the chick pushes its way out.

## Other Babies
## Are Not Quite as Helpless

Baby chicks are born from eggs which the mother hen lays. She sits on her eggs for three weeks. This keeps them warm while great changes take place. Inside the eggs, baby chicks are forming and growing strong enough to be hatched.

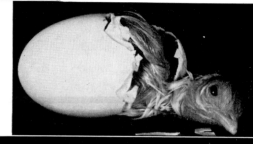

At first its feathers are wet, and it is too weak to stand up.

But in just a few hours its feathers are dry and fluffy. And it is strong enough to run about and hunt for food.

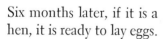

In three weeks, it looks like this.

Six months later, if it is a hen, it is ready to lay eggs.

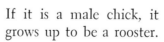

If it is a male chick, it grows up to be a rooster.

You can see that a baby chick doesn't need as much care as a puppy, a kitten, or a baby rabbit does.

W. F. Lamoreux, Dept. of
Poultry Husbandry,
Cornell University

## Still Other Baby Animals Are Left to Take Care of Themselves

When the baby animals shown on this page are born, they have to take care of themselves. After their mothers lay the eggs, they give the babies no care at all.

But these babies are not as helpless as puppies, kittens, and baby rabbits. Just as soon as they are born, they know how to get food, how to move about, and how to hide from danger.

When baby turtles hatch from eggs that their mother has laid, they must take care of themselves.

Lynwood M. Chace

Frogs have to take care of themselves as soon as they hatch from eggs into little tadpoles like these.

Baby fishes have to take care of themselves, too. And so do most insects.

Do you know of any other animal babies which have to take care of themselves just as soon as they are born?

## Many Baby Animals Learn from Their Mothers

Many animal babies learn by watching their mothers. They try to do what their mothers do.

Seals spend most of their time in water. But baby seals cannot swim! They must be taught to swim by their mothers.

This mother raccoon teaches its baby many things that it must know.

The mother deer teaches its baby to lie quietly in hiding and to run from danger. The baby needs to know how to run away and hide. If it did not learn this, it might be killed by other animals.

The mother polar bear also teaches its cub many things it must know.

Wide World; Kirkpatrick, Nowell, Black Star

Can you think of other animal babies that learn things from their parents?

You learn by watching your parents do things, just as baby animals do.

## Boys and Girls Learn Much More than Animal Babies Can

You know more than the smartest animal that ever lived. You are smarter than the smartest animal. You can learn more by asking questions and by understanding what others are doing and talking about. Animals cannot read or write or think as you can. They are not curious about the world as you are.

You learn by watching other people do things. You also learn by watching things happen and by thinking about what you have seen.

You learn how to do things by asking questions, too.

Ewing Galloway; H. Armstrong Roberts

And you learn by reading, or by being read to. You can learn from people that lived long ago, and from people in other lands, because they wrote about what they thought and knew. Animal babies cannot do any of these things.

15

## Some Babies Look Altogether Different from Their Parents

Did you ever see a baby camel at a zoo or a circus? It looks just like a grown-up camel, only smaller. But there are some babies that do not look like their parents at all.

1 Did you ever see a caterpillar like this one? Do you know what it really is? It is a baby butterfly!

Brownell; Lynwood M. Chace; Spencer

2 Here is its mother! It is a Monarch butterfly. Some day, the caterpillar will change to look just like this. How can a butterfly have a caterpillar baby? How can a caterpillar grow up to be a butterfly?

3 The mother butterfly lays its eggs on a milkweed or other plant.

4 The eggs hatch into tiny caterpillars. Here is a caterpillar that has just hatched. It eats and eats and grows and grows. From time to time, the growing caterpillar gets too big for its skin. When this happens, the skin splits up the back and the caterpillar crawls right out. Then it grows a new skin. This happens several times.

5  Then, one day, the caterpillar fastens itself to a twig and makes a hard case to cover itself. Then it looks like this.

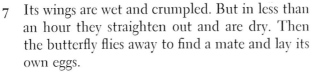

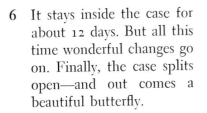

6  It stays inside the case for about 12 days. But all this time wonderful changes go on. Finally, the case splits open—and out comes a beautiful butterfly.

7  Its wings are wet and crumpled. But in less than an hour they straighten out and are dry. Then the butterfly flies away to find a mate and lay its own eggs.

Brownell; Halliday; Jenkins; Spencer

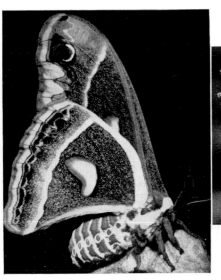

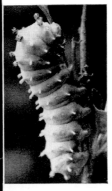

Baby moths also look different from their parents, as you can see by looking at these pictures. Butterflies and moths are called *insects*. There are many kinds of insects. Most insect babies look different from their parents.

17

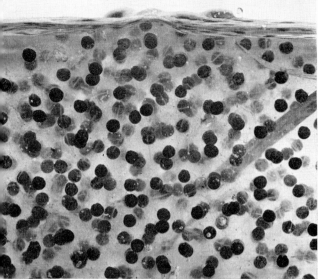

## Frog Babies Look Different, Too

Insect babies are not the only ones that look different from their parents. Frog babies do not look at all like grown-up frogs.

The mother frog lays its eggs in the water. They look like this.

Each egg changes and changes.

In about eight days, each egg hatches into a tadpole. It is a baby frog, but it does not look like its mother. Do you see the featherlike things? They are gills. The tadpole can breathe under water with them.

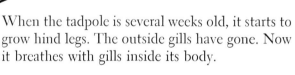

When the tadpole is several weeks old, it starts to grow hind legs. The outside gills have gone. Now it breathes with gills inside its body.

As time goes on, its tail gets smaller and smaller, and it grows front legs.

Then its tail disappears, and it has changed into a grown-up frog. It now can live out of water and catch insects. Its gills are gone and it breathes with **lungs** just as you do.

18

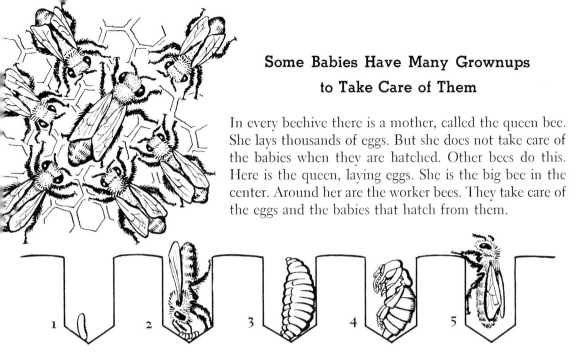

## Some Babies Have Many Grownups
## to Take Care of Them

In every beehive there is a mother, called the queen bee. She lays thousands of eggs. But she does not take care of the babies when they are hatched. Other bees do this. Here is the queen, laying eggs. She is the big bee in the center. Around her are the worker bees. They take care of the eggs and the babies that hatch from them.

Each egg (1) hatches into a tiny wormlike grub. Here is a grub in its little wax home that a worker bee built.

Each grub (2) eats the food the worker bees bring to it. It grows (3), sheds its skin, and eats some more. Then it changes into a pupa (4).

After a while the pupa changes into a grown-up bee (5).

The bee crawls out of its home, dries its wings, and begins its work in the hive. Ant babies are cared for by many grownups, too.

## Be Your Own Zoo Keeper

How would you like to be a zoo keeper? You can start by keeping insects. It is fun to collect insects and watch how they live. Here is what you should do.

Ask your mother or father to help you make a net for catching the insects. You will need . . .

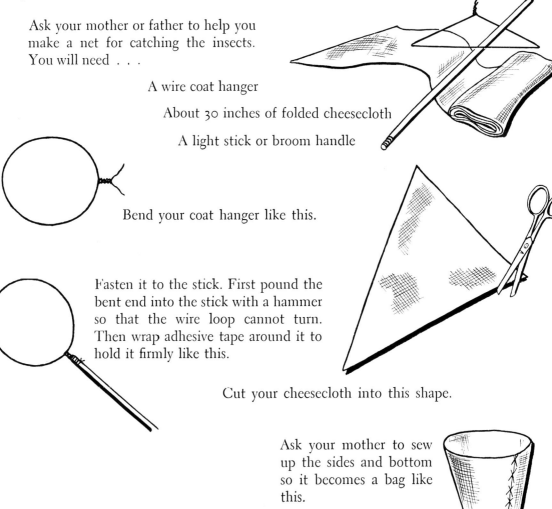

A wire coat hanger

About 30 inches of folded cheesecloth

A light stick or broom handle

Bend your coat hanger like this.

Fasten it to the stick. First pound the bent end into the stick with a hammer so that the wire loop cannot turn. Then wrap adhesive tape around it to hold it firmly like this.

Cut your cheesecloth into this shape.

Ask your mother to sew up the sides and bottom so it becomes a bag like this.

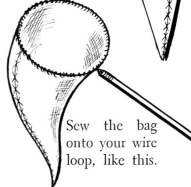

Sew the bag onto your wire loop, like this.

Now you are ready to catch insects for your zoo.

## Your Zoo Cage

But where will you put the insects you catch? A zoo keeper needs a cage for his animals.

To make a good cage, you will need two pie tins. You will also need a piece of window screen about 6 inches wide and three times as long as the width of your pie tins.

Bend your screen into a circle like this. Fasten the ends together with a needle and thread.

Place the screen in a pie tin. Ask Dad to cut a piece of sod just large enough to fit into the pie tin. Perhaps he can get it from a corner of your lawn or an open field. Then cover the top of the cage with the other pie tin. Your insect cage is complete.

Now you can go hunting to get insects for your zoo. Take your net and a quart jar with a cover. You will find insects almost everywhere except in winter. You can always find them in the park or in a field of tall grass. Sweep your net through the grass and put the insects you catch in your jar.

You will find caterpillars and other insects on trees, flowers, and bushes. Be sure to take some of the leaves from the plant where you find the caterpillars, for they may not eat anything else.

When you get home, put the insects into your zoo cage. Now you can watch them close at hand. Keep the sod moist by sprinkling it with water. After you have enjoyed your insects for a few days, let them go. Why?

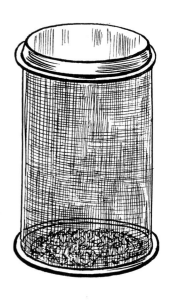

The dragonfly has four large wings which you can see through.

Here is the small white cabbage butterfly. Its caterpillar eats leaves of cabbage, broccoli, and Brussels sprouts. It causes much damage to our gardens.

Gluck, National Audubon Society; Hillman; Howard

And you will surely find crickets. They "sing" by rubbing their wings together. You will hear their song if you listen on a summer's night. Baby crickets look like their parents, too.

You will find many kinds of interesting beetles. Each has a hard case over its thin wings. Do you see the wing cover on this June bug?

22

The caterpillar of the beautiful sphinx moth is called a tomato, or tobacco worm, because it feeds on these plants.

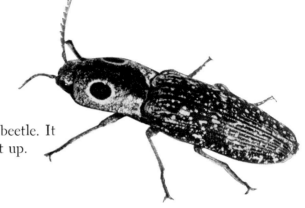

Here is the interesting click beetle. It goes "click" when you pick it up.

Jenkins; Howard; Ewing Galloway

You will find grasshoppers almost anywhere. Baby grasshoppers look just like their parents, only smaller.

This is a golden garden spider. It can be found in many gardens.

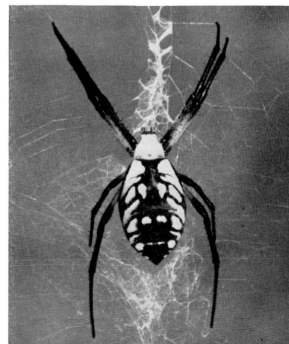

Do not try to pick up a bee or a wasp, for it will sting and hurt you.

## Where Do Plants Come From?

Trees, bushes, vegetables, and other plants have parents, just as animals do. But they are not born from a mother, as a baby kitten is. They do not hatch from eggs, as chickens and insects do. They come from seeds.

Orville Logan Snider

How would you like to grow some plants of your own?

Ask your mother to give you some dried beans. These are the seeds of bean plants. Seeds are something like the eggs of animals. New plants grow from them.

Soak the beans in water over night. The skins get soft and wrinkled like this . . .

Now peel off the skin of one bean. The skinned bean has two main parts. Can you pull these two halves carefully apart?

Look closely inside. What was between the two parts? A baby plant! Can you see the tiny leaves? A magnifying glass will help you to see the baby plant better.

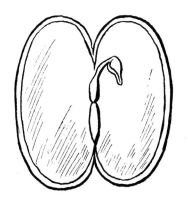

A seed is really the beginning of a baby plant, together with stored food. The food in the bean seed is stored in the two halves.

## What Happens
## When You Plant Bean Seeds?

To find the answer, you will need about five soaked bean seeds, a drinking glass, and a piece of blotting paper, rolled so it fits inside the glass like this . . .

Place your bean seeds between the blotter and the glass so that the blotter holds them in place, like this . . .

Pour about an inch of water into the glass. The water will soak the blotter and will keep the seeds moist. Plants cannot grow unless they have water.

Now wrap a paper around the outside of the glass and fasten it with a rubber band. This keeps light away from the seeds. Seeds are usually planted in the ground where it is dark.

Place your glass in a warm place. Seeds need warmth to grow, but they will be killed if it is too hot. And they will not grow if it is too cold. Every few days, take off the outside paper and see how much your beans have grown. Then put the paper back on again.

Do you see how the roots go down and the stem grows up? Do you see how the two halves of the seed are carried up by the stem? The plant uses the stored food in these two parts until it can get its own food.

## Do Plants Grow Only from Seeds?

Let's experiment and find out!

Place a sweet potato in a glass of water. Put the glass in a warm, sunny place. Soon, little buds appear. These become stems, and leaves grow from the stems. If you keep water in the glass you will soon have a beautiful plant.

You can grow a carrot plant by cutting a piece about an inch thick off the top of a carrot. Cut off the leaves and put the carrot piece, with the top up, in a pan. Put the pan in a warm, sunny place. In a few days, look to see what is happening.

Fenner

You can also ask your mother to cut a thick, green piece from a geranium plant for you. Place it in a glass about one third full of water. After a while, this will grow roots. Then you can put it in a flowerpot in dirt and it will grow into a new plant.

## Seeds Which Are Not Really Seeds

Some plants grow from tiny things that act like seeds, but are really not seeds at all. These tiny things are called *spores*. They are made by the parent plant.

Mushrooms grow from spores.

So does moss. The tiny balls you see are full of spores.

Ferns also come from spores. The spots on the underneath sides of the leaves are full of spores.

Spencer; Gottscho-Schleisner

### Grow Your Own Spores

Ask Mother for a glass jar with a tin lid. Place a piece of wet paper towel in the bottom of the jar. Now put a piece of fresh white bread in the jar.

Punch a few holes in the jar lid and put it on the jar. Place the jar in a warm, dark place for a week or more. The bread will become covered with a white mold with blue or black spots.

This mold is a plant which grows from spores instead of from seeds. The spores are made in the tiny blue or black spots that you can see. These spots are tiny cases full of even tinier spores. The cases break open and the tiny spores float around in the air. They are too little to see, but, if they alight on bread or other food, they may start to grow.

27

# What Do Plants and Animals Need to Live and Grow?

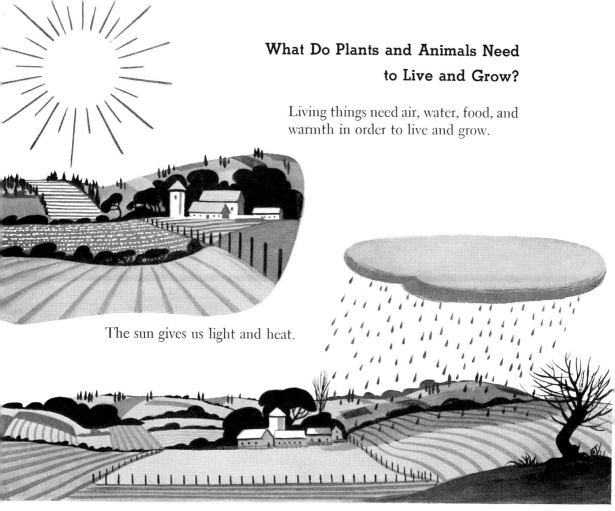

Living things need air, water, food, and warmth in order to live and grow.

The sun gives us light and heat.

The earth we live on gives us air, water, and food.

Let us see how plants and animals get some of the things they need to live and grow!

## How Do Living Things
## Get the Air They Need?

Air is very important. Without air to breathe, people, plants, and animals would die.

You breathe air through your nose or mouth. It is better to breathe through your nose, for this helps to warm and clean the air before it goes to your lungs.

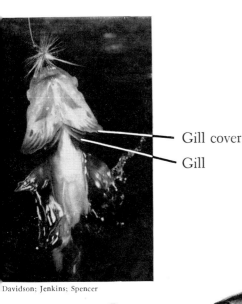

— Gill cover

— Gill

Davidson; Jenkins; Spencer

Fish can breathe the air that is dissolved in water. They do not have lungs, such as you have. Instead, they have feathery things, called *gills*, just as tadpoles do. A fish's gills are at the sides of its head. The water goes in the fish's mouth, past the gills where the air is taken out, and then out the side of the fish's head.

Insects have neither lungs nor gills. Air goes in through openings along the sides of their bodies. These openings connect with tiny tubes inside.

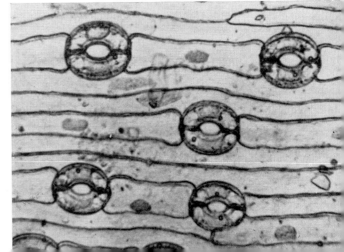

Plants must have air, too. The leaves take in air through tiny holes that are usually on the underside.

29

## Where Do Living Things Get the Food They Need?

Your food comes from both plants and anim⎡

Vegetables and fruits come from plants.

Such foods as meat an⎤ milk come from an⎤ mals.

From the milk of cow⎤ we get butter an⎤ cheese.

Even bread and breakfast cereals are made from wheat, corn, barley, rye, and rice.

Some animals, like this mountain lion, eat only meat.

Others, including sheep, eat only plants.

30

## All Food
## Really Comes from Green Plants

If it were not for green plants, all people and all animals in the world would soon starve to death! This is because green plants make food. You cannot make food. Nor can animals. So people and animals must depend largely upon green plants for the food they eat.

Even when you eat meat, you are really eating food made by plants.

This rooster eats corn and other food. It will grow big because it eats the food which plants make.

So when you eat roast beef, or a piece of chicken, or any kind of meat, you are really eating plant food that was changed by an animal's body into meat.

H. Armstrong Roberts; Jenkins; Lambert

## How Do Green Plants Make Their Food?

A green plant takes water from the ground and a gas from the air. With the help of light, it makes sugar out of the water and the gas. Then it adds things called minerals that it gets from the ground through its roots, and makes many other kinds of foods.

water and gas

light

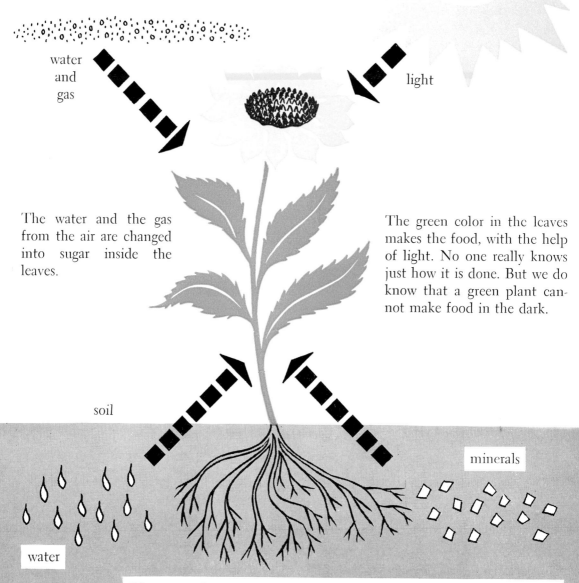

The water and the gas from the air are changed into sugar inside the leaves.

The green color in the leaves makes the food, with the help of light. No one really knows just how it is done. But we do know that a green plant cannot make food in the dark.

soil

minerals

water

The green plant gets the water and minerals it needs to make food from the soil in which it grows. The minerals dissolve in the water. The water goes into the roots and up the stem and into the leaves.

You can see that green plants are really food factories. They make food for themselves, for animals, and for people.

## How Does Water Get Up into the Leaves?

Here is an interesting experiment for you to try.

Ask your mother for a stalk of celery with leaves on it.

Put about two inches of water into a glass. Pour a little red ink or mercurochrome into the water. The ink dissolves in the water just as minerals dissolve in water in the ground. Now put the celery stalk into the glass.

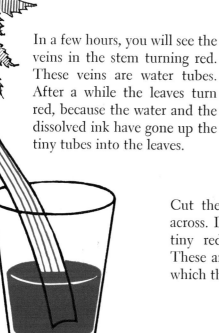

In a few hours, you will see the veins in the stem turning red. These veins are water tubes. After a while the leaves turn red, because the water and the dissolved ink have gone up the tiny tubes into the leaves.

Cut the stem straight across. Do you see the tiny red spots in it?
These are the ends of the tiny tubes through which the water traveled upward to the leaves.

Now cut a piece of the stem like this. Do you see the tiny tubes with the red water in them?

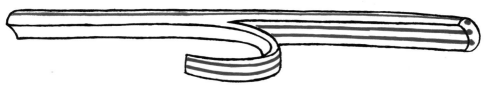

When a plant grows in the soil, its roots soak up water and minerals that are dissolved in the water. The tiny tubes carry the water and minerals up to the leaves.

## What Happens to the Food a Plant Makes?

All plants make food so that they can live and grow. What happens to all this food? Where is it stored?

lettuce

cabbage

spinach

Ylla, Rapho-Guillumette

Some of the food stays in the leaves. Cows and sheep eat blades of grass. Rabbits like to eat the leaves of our garden plants.

Cabbage, spinach, and garden lettuce are some of the leaves which you eat.

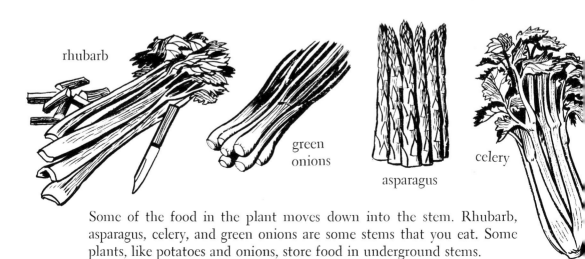

rhubarb

green onions

asparagus

celery

Some of the food in the plant moves down into the stem. Rhubarb, asparagus, celery, and green onions are some stems that you eat. Some plants, like potatoes and onions, store food in underground stems.

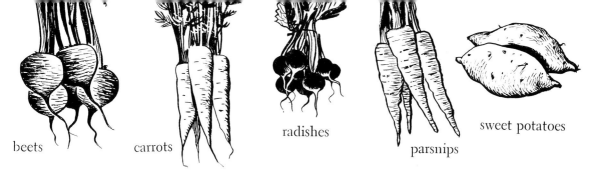

beets   carrots   radishes   parsnips   sweet potatoes

All green plants move some of their food down into their roots. Many plants, like carrots, parsnips, beets, radishes, and sweet potatoes, store most of their food in a big storage root.

broccoli

A few plants make flowers which you eat. Among these is broccoli.

The sweet nectar of flowers is the only food of grown-up butterflies and moths.

pears

tomatoes   plums

You eat the fruit of many plants, such as apples, plums, tomatoes, and pears.

All green plants store food in their seeds. You eat nuts, beans, and peas. These are all seeds.

beans

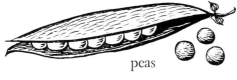

peas

nuts

What other plants which you eat store food in leaves, stems, roots, fruits, flowers, or seeds?

## How Do Leaves Grow on Trees?

Each spring, new leaves form on the trees. All winter long the branches have been bare. What happens to make leaves form? Where do they come from? Try this, and see!

In the springtime cut a twig from a horse chestnut, a pussy willow, or other tree. Look carefully at your twig for the little tips which stick out. These are called buds. Leaves and flowers come from buds. You can watch the buds change into leaves. Some may change into flowers. Place your twig in a glass of water.

After a time, you will see the buds begin to swell. They keep on swelling until the covers on the buds begin to split and fall off.

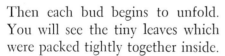

Then each bud begins to unfold. You will see the tiny leaves which were packed tightly together inside.

Spencer; J. Horace McFarland Co.

Finally, the leaves open wide and begin to grow larger until they are fully grown in summer. They are the tree's food factory.

Before the leaves drop in the fall, trees make tiny new buds that are tightly packed. All winter long these baby leaves are protected by the bud covers, until spring comes again. Then they unfold and begin their work of making food for the tree.

Gottscho-Schleisner; J. Horace McFarland Co.

## Why Do Leaves Turn Color and Drop in the Fall?

Did you ever wonder why leaves turn color and drop in the fall? It is the tree's way of protecting itself in the winter and of getting ready for spring. Here is what happens.

All summer long, each green leaf makes food for the plant. It is green because it is full of the green-colored matter with which it makes food.

But, underneath the green color, the leaf is really yellow, orange, or perhaps red. When the leaf stops working in autumn, no more water comes to it. The green color fades away and the other colors show through with the bright yellows and reds of fall.

By late fall, all the food has been taken out of the leaf. It is now stored in the fruits, stems, seeds, or roots. The old leaf has done its work and is of no use to the tree any more. It slowly dies. The tree loosens the dead leaf and it drops to the ground. Now the tree is ready for winter.

37

## How Do Animals Protect Themselves?

Animals have to eat to keep alive. But they could not live long if they could not protect themselves from other animals that want to eat them. Some animals depend on speed to protect themselves from their enemies.

A jack rabbit cannot fight back. But it can run at a speed of about 45 miles an hour.

The gazelle can leap along even faster, at 60 miles an hour. Your car would have to go fast to keep up with it.

A flying fish can rush through the water at about 35 miles an hour. It also can leap out of the water and sail through the air on its winglike fins.

J. C. Allen and Son; Wide World; Edgerton, National Audubon Society; Spencer; Chicago Natural History Museum

When the cat is around, the mouse will run fast for its hole in the wall.

The mountain goat also uses its speed to escape its enemies.

## Color and Shape
## Help to Protect Some Animals

Look carefully! The animal in this picture is an insect called a walking stick. It looks just like a twig on the tree.

This is an Arctic fox. In winter, when the ground is covered with snow and ice, its brownish summer coat turns pure white. This makes it difficult to see.

The leopard is hard to see against the sun-spotted shadows of its jungle home.

rownell; New York Zoological Society; Pinney, Monkmeyer; Black Star; Ylla, Rapho-Guillumette

The zebra's stripes blend with the open grassy plains of Africa, where it lives.

The chameleon is hard to see. It changes its color to match its surroundings.

## Other Animals
## Have Weapons
## to Protect Themselves

Some animals, like this moose, have antlers or horns.

Lanks, Monkmeyer; Ewing Galloway; Ylla, Rapho-Guillumett

Some animals, such as the eagle, have sharp claws.

So does your kitten have sharp claws. Usually its claws are tucked away in its paws so that they won't scratch. But, when it wants to, it can stick them away out like this.

The rhinoceros has a horn on its nose, which makes a useful weapon.

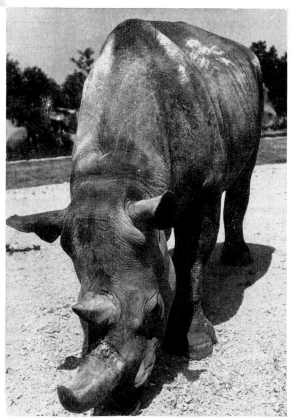

## These Animals Fight with Their Feet

Claws aren't the only weapons used by animals that fight with their feet.

Horses fight by kicking. Their hooves are really big toenails. They are hard and can crush a small animal. Deer fight with their front feet in the same way when they are cornered. Their tiny hooves are sharp and dangerous.

The ostrich can kick with an awful wallop.

Owen, Black Star; Ylla, Rapho-Guillumette

And so can the kangaroo.

This wolf has sharp teeth called fangs.

Look at the fangs on this black leopard!

. . . and on this Bengal tiger!

## These Animals Fight with Their Teeth

Some animals use their teeth for catching food. Others use their teeth for chewing food. Still other animals have special teeth for fighting.

Some animals, like this elephant, grow extra long teeth called tusks.

The wart hog, a fierce wild pig which lives in Africa, also has tusks.

The shark has several rows of long sharp teeth.

The oyster has a hard shell to protect itself from many of its enemies.

**Some Animals Have Armor**

The snail can hide in its shell.

And so can the conch.

The armadillo also has a bony shell covering for its body.

Brownell; Howard; Lynwood M. Chace; Brown Bros.; New York Zoological Society

This porcupine fish swallows air or water, and blows itself up big so that it looks like a prickly pincushion.

## Many Animals Use Poison

Most snakes in the United States are not poisonous. They are harmless. They should not be hurt, for they kill mice and other harmful animals.

This is the harmless garter snake.

### Four Kinds of Poisonous Snakes

rattlesnake

copperhead

There are four kinds of snakes in the United States which are poisonous. Their fangs are hollow and are connected to sacs full of poison. When they bite, the poison is squeezed into the holes made by the fangs. Keep away from these snakes. It is safer for you not to pick up **any** snakes.

water moccasin

coral snake

The skunk protects itself by squirting a bad-smelling fluid at its enemies.

This porcupine's body is covered with stiff quills which have barbs on the ends.

## Other Animal Weapons

### Animals Use Weapons to Get Food

This is a Portuguese man-of-war. The long things hanging down are filled with tiny poison darts. They are used to help it catch small fishes.

This archerfish has a kind of built-in water pistol. It squirts water at insects and then gobbles them up when they drop into the water.

45

## Do Plants Protect Themselves?

A rose plant protects itself with sharp thorns.

The cactus and other plants have prickly spines.

The skunk cabbage has a nasty smell.

The poison ivy contains an oil which will make you itch.

Would you want to pull up this bull thistle? Why not?

H. Armstrong Roberts; Brown Bros.;
J. Horace McFarland Co.; Brownell

## Where Do Animals Live?

Animals build all kinds of homes. Some have their homes on the ground and some on the water. Some build homes underground and some under the water. Still others have their homes in trees and on mountaintops and cliffs. Most fish do not have homes. Nor do most snakes, turtles, and insects.

The eagle often builds its nest on a craggy peak or tall tree, where it is safe from its enemies.

The grebe, a bird, builds a floating nest on the water among weeds and cattails.

Brownell; Lynwood M. Chace; Ewing Galloway

The meadow lark builds its nest on the ground in fields and open places.

The clam burrows into the sand.

The brook stickleback is rare among fishes, for it builds a nest of plants under water.

The lizard makes its home in a hole among rocks.

The badger lives in a hole in the ground.

So does the ground hog.

## Underground Homes

And the coyote digs tunnels into the earth. It hides the entrance in bushes or rocks.

Bears find caves in which they can spend the winter sleeping. Here, too, is where they have their babies.

The river otter makes its home in the banks along streams.

## Don't Bother This Home!

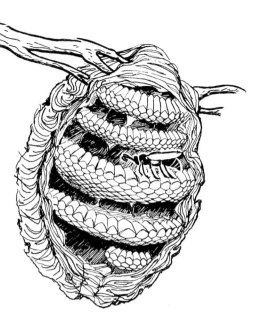

A family of wasps lives here. Wasps can sting!

This is what the nest looks like inside. It is a sort of paper apartment house. Eggs are laid in the paper cells. Each egg hatches into a baby grub that eats the food the worker wasps put into the cell with it. Later, it changes into a full-grown wasp.

### How Wasps Make Their Nest

In building their nest, wasps chew up wood to make a kind of paper. They pat the paper around with their mouths to make a little roof for the nest. They fasten this roof to a tree or something solid.

Then they make a sort of paper honeycomb—then another—and then another. Each is fastened to the one above it. And the nest is covered with a paperlike material.

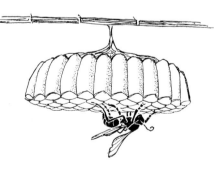

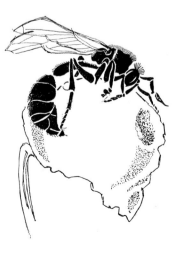

Some kinds of wasps just make a paper comb and don't cover it with paper. Other kinds of wasps live alone and make nests like this, out of mud.

49

# Make Your Own Home for Water Animals and Plants

It is fun to make a home for fish, snails, and water plants. Such a home is called an aquarium. You can have one for your house. Then you will have fun watching the animals and plants in their water home.

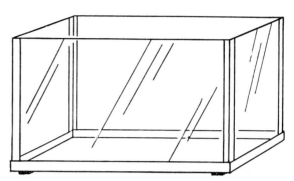

You can have any size or shape of aquarium that you want. You can buy it in a pet store. Or, perhaps, your father knows how to make one.

After you buy or make the aquarium, you will need some clean sand from the beach or from your sandbox. This should be carefully washed. You need enough to cover the bottom of the aquarium to a depth of two inches.

You also will need water plants. There are many kinds which you can buy at a pet shop.

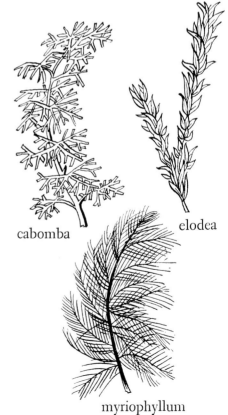

cabomba

elodea

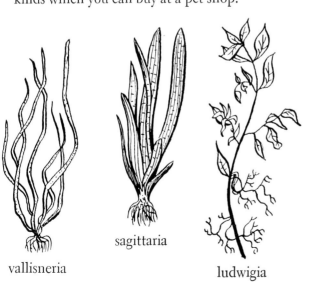

vallisneria

sagittaria

ludwigia

myriophyllum

ram's-horn
snail

Japanese
snail

Australian
red
snail

pond
snail

You can probably find all the snails you need in a near-by pond. If not, you can buy them at a pet store. Get about twelve. Here are some of the kinds you can buy.

You can get fish from a pet shop, too, but it is lots more fun to catch your own. You can make a small net like the one shown on page 20, and try to net some tiny fish at a lake, river, or big pond. Here are some common small fish you may be able to catch in your net.

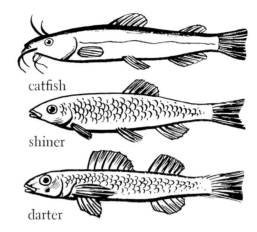
catfish

shiner

darter

sunfish

An eight-gallon aquarium is large enough for about eight fish that are about one inch long. Plan on having about one gallon of water for each inch of fish.

When you have made your aquarium, it will look something like this. Set it where it will get about six hours of bright light a day. But don't let it get much direct sunlight or soon it will be full of green scum, which is a kind of water plant. You can get dried insects and other kinds of fish food at a pet shop. You should feed the fish not more than two or three times a week. Do not feed them too much or too often. The food not eaten will turn the water sour.

## Making Your Own Home for Land Animals and Plants

How would you like to set up a terrarium—a home for land animals and plants? A terrarium is like an aquarium, except that it has soil instead of water. It also has land plants and animals.

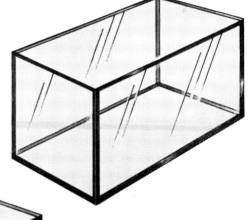

First, you should get a large glass container, something like your aquarium. A large glass jar will do, if you put a piece of glass on top for a cover.

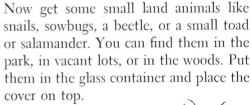

Put a layer of sand or gravel about an inch thick on the bottom. Then put two inches of good soil on top of the sand or gravel. If you like, you can add a small log, a rock, or stone.

Plant moss, small ferns, and a little grass sod in the soil. Be sure to add water to the soil.

Now get some small land animals like snails, sowbugs, a beetle, or a small toad or salamander. You can find them in the park, in vacant lots, or in the woods. Put them in the glass container and place the cover on top.

snail

beetle

sowbug

toad

salamander

The terrarium will need no care for a long time, if the cover is put on tightly. The cover will keep the water from escaping and the soil from drying. The water will evaporate from the soil, but it will form drops on the bottom of the cover and fall back down like rain.

Be sure to keep the terrarium out of the direct sunlight, or it might get too hot.

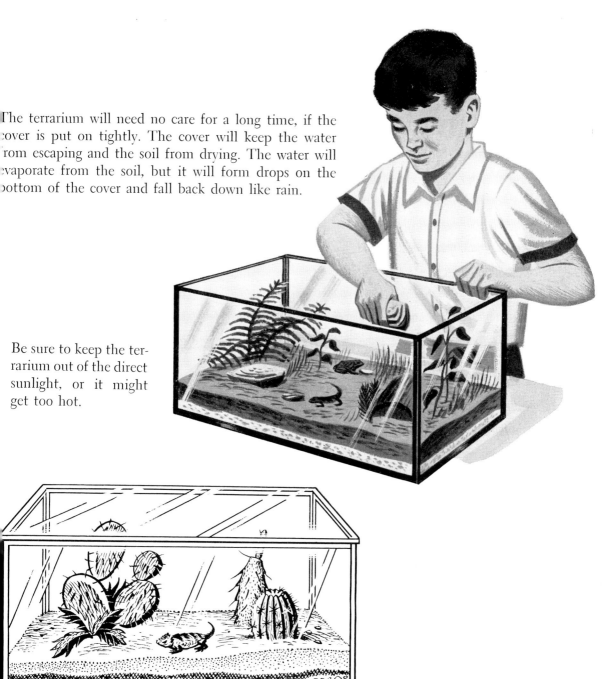

A Desert Terrarium

You can make all sorts of terrariums. If you use very sandy soil and don't keep it too wet, you can make an interesting desert terrarium with small cactuses you can buy at a florist shop or at the ten-cent store. It may look something like this.

ocean

craggy peaks

river

jungle

ice floe

desert

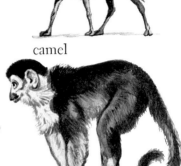

camel

monkey

mountain goat

polar bear

hippopotamus

whale

## Which Belongs with Which?

You have seen that animals have different kinds of homes. An animal that lives in the ocean needs a different kind of home from that of an animal that lives on the land. An animal that lives in the hot, dry desert needs a different kind of home from that of an animal that lives in the snow-covered Northland.

On this page are shown the pictures of a number of different animals and the places where they live. Can you tell in what place each animal lives?

# The People
# Who Live in the World

Men and women and children live in almost every part of the world. They do not all look alike. Nor do they live in the same way.

Some have white skins. Others have black skins. Still others are brown or yellow. The color and shape of their hair and eyes may be different. They may not eat the same things or dress in the same way.

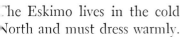

The Eskimo lives in the cold North and must dress warmly.

Our American Indians who live in the hot deserts wear little clothing.

But, actually, people are much the same wherever they may live. They differ from animals in many ways. They are much more intelligent, for they can think and speak and write. They have minds and souls, which animals do not have. Faith is an important part of man's life, even though all peoples do not worship in the same way.

The pygmy tribes in the hot jungles need little clothing.

Harrington, Matter, Black Star; Monkmeyer; H. Armstrong Roberts; Gendreau; Woody Williams

Some of the people in the South Pacific islands have fuzzy hair.

Many people in India wear turbans.

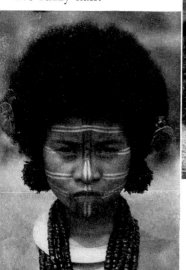

The Arabs wear long flowing robes.

55

## Different Peoples Have Different Homes

In the cold Northland, many Eskimos live in snow igloos in winter and in skin tents in summer.

Hansen, Black Star

Many of the Arabs live in tents.

These Korean children live in houses with straw roofs.

Some Indian families still live in tepees.

In the African jungles, people have houses that keep out the hot sun and let the breeze through.

H. Armstrong Roberts

You will find houses on stilts in the faraway islands of the Pacific Ocean.

Here are other kinds of houses. Can you tell about still other kinds of houses?

## What Kinds of Plants Are There in the World?

There are many, many different kinds of plants in the world. But there are only four main groups.

One group includes the mushrooms, toadstools, molds, and the tiny yeasts and bacteria. Yeasts and bacteria are so small they can't be seen except under a microscope.

The mosses make up another group.

Another group includes the ferns. Long before there were bushes and trees, there were great forests of giant ferns.

Brownell; Spencer; Gottscho-Schleisner

There is also a group that includes plants which have flowers. Among these are trees, bushes, weeds, grasses, cereals, and all the other plants we raise for food or for their beautiful flowers. This is the group of plants which we know best.

57

## What Kinds of Animals Are There in the World?

Just as there are many kinds of plants, so, too, there are many kinds of animals in the world. They are found almost everywhere. No one person could possibly know them all. But you can always remember that there are two big groups—the animals which have backbones, and the animals which have no backbones.

### Some Animals Which Have No Backbones

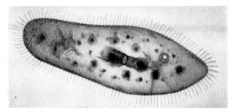

There are animals so tiny that thousands can live in one drop of water. You cannot even see them without a strong microscope. Here are two common ones which have no backbones.

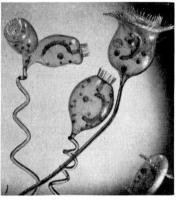

Worms, such as this large earthworm called the night crawler, have no backbones.

The octopus, a sea animal, has a soft body and eight huge tentacles, but it has no backbone.

Nor do thousands of different kinds of shell animals, such as this clam, that live on the seashore.

Nor does the sponge, a sea animal whose skeleton we use for washing the car.

Rochester Museum of Arts and Sciences; Bausch and Lomb; Howard; Ewing Galloway; Woody Williams

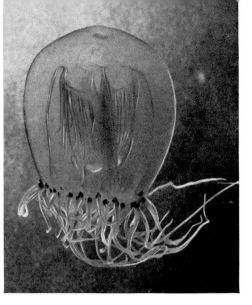

This jellyfish has no backbone either. But it can swim through the water by pushing its umbrella up and down.

The spiny-skinned starfish is yet another sea animal which has no backbone.

### Animals with Jointed Legs

Several kinds of animals have jointed legs. They do not have backbones, but their bodies have a hard cover which makes a kind of outside skeleton.

spider

Spiders, cockroaches, and beetles have no backbones.

cockroach

beetle

All insects, such as this praying mantis, have no backbones.

Woody Williams; Hibbs; Howard

Nor does the centipede, sometimes called a thousand-legged worm.

crayfish

The lobster, crab, and crayfish are shellfish which have no backbones.

crab

59

## Animals Which Have Backbones

This is a haddock. All kinds of fishes have backbones.

So do toads, frogs, and salamanders.

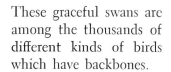

Chicago Natural History Museum; Jenkins;
Century Photos; Rowe, Black Star; Lynwood M. Chace

Scaly-skinned reptiles, like this horned toad, have backbones, too.

These graceful swans are among the thousands of different kinds of birds which have backbones.

## Animals Which Give Milk to Their Babies

Yet another group of animals which have backbones are the mammals. These animals give milk to their young, and are good parents. They usually have hair or bristles on their bodies.

The giraffe is the tallest of all animals. But its neck has the same number of bones as does the neck of the smallest mouse.

Ylla, Rapho-Guillumette; Wide World; Chicago Natural History Museum; Lynwood M. Chace

The baby kangaroo is very tiny when born. It lives in its mother's pouch until it can take care of itself.

The opossum takes its babies for a piggyback ride when they are old enough.

This mother raccoon is carrying its baby to a place of safety.

## Some Plants and Animals Are too Small to Be Seen!

Why does your mother insist that you wash your hands before you eat? Isn't that a funny question to ask when you are learning about plants and animals? Well—not really! Do you know why?

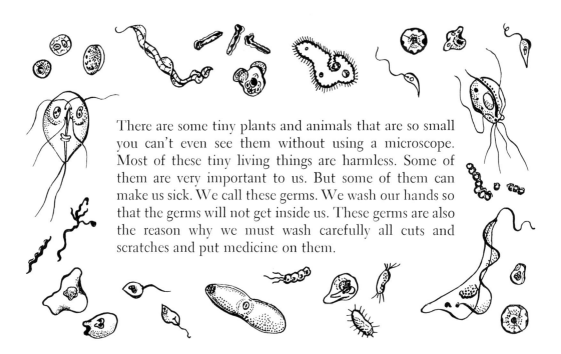

There are some tiny plants and animals that are so small you can't even see them without using a microscope. Most of these tiny living things are harmless. Some of them are very important to us. But some of them can make us sick. We call these germs. We wash our hands so that the germs will not get inside us. These germs are also the reason why we must wash carefully all cuts and scratches and put medicine on them.

That is why, too, we brush our teeth after eating, and why we take baths. To keep well, it is important that we keep clean.

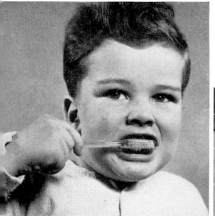

H. Armstrong Roberts

The pictures on this page show what some germs look like under the microscope. They are all much too tiny for us to see without a microscope.

## Let's Try an Experiment!

Ask your mother for three apples—two good ones, and one with a rotten spot on it.

Touch the rotten spot of the first apple to the skin of one of the good apples.

Scratch the skin of the third apple in two places with a fork. Touch the rotten spot of the first apple to both scratched places. Then put iodine or mercurochrome on one of the two scratches. Then watch the three apples for a few days.

**Here is what probably will happen . . .**

The rotten apple will be more rotten.

The apple with the unscratched skin will be more or less the same.

The scratched apple will begin to rot in the scratch which was not treated with medicine. The other scratch will not rot so soon.

What does this tell you about an apple's skin? Germs make things rot. But an apple's skin helps to keep out the germs. Do you suppose your skin acts in the same way? Your skin protects you against disease germs that might get inside you. It is important to take care of all cuts and scratches quickly.

63

## Plants and Animals Depend on Each Other

All animals depend on plants for their food in one way or another.

Plants also provide shelter for a great many animals, and nesting places for birds.

Animals help plants, too. They carry seeds which plants make to other places where new plants grow.

Bees carry pollen from flower to flower on fruit trees, so they will bear fruit. Have you ever seen pollen? It is the yellow powder you will find in flowers.

Without the bumble-bee to carry pollen, red clover would not grow.

Jenkins; Lambert; J. C. Allen and Son; Century Photos

Other insects also carry pollen from flower to flower.

# How Plants and Animals Help Us

Animals and plants furnish us with all kinds of food which we can eat and enjoy.

Both plants and animals provide many materials from which the clothes we wear are made.

Even the homes we live in could not be built and furnished without materials provided by our animal and plant friends.

Animals and plants are also used by people in all parts of the world to help them with their work, and to take them from one place to another.

In India and other countries, the elephant is used to move heavy things.

In Peru and other South American countries, the llama works for man.

The Eskimo's dogs make it possible for him to travel far and fast over the snowy places of the Far North.

Ewing Galloway; Gendreau; Harrington, Black Star

The camel is used by man in North Africa and parts of Asia. Other animals used in different places to help man with his work are the yak, the water buffalo, and the donkey.

# THE EARTH
# WE LIVE ON

James Sawders, Cushing

67

## What the Earth Is Like

Did you ever wonder what the earth is like? It looks different in different places. These places are like each other in some ways. They are quite different in other ways.

What is the shape of the earth? Does the sun really rise and set? Why do we have spring, summer, fall, and winter? What makes things fall? And why does it rain and snow?

Why does the wind blow? And what use do we make of air, soil, and water? What makes thunder and lightning? And how can we tell direction?

These and other questions are answered on the pages that follow. You will find many interesting things to do. They will help you to understand this wonderful world in which we live.

## High Lands of the Earth

You can only see a small part of the earth from where you live. All parts of the world are not the same as that part of it which you can see.

Many parts of the world have high lands and mountains. Some mountains rise for miles into the sky. They are covered with snow and no trees or plants grow on them.

Courtesy *Life*, © Time, Inc.

This is the highest mountain in the world. It is Mount Everest, near faraway India.

Some hills and mountains, such as these in New York, are covered with forests of various kinds.

New York Dept. of Conservation
Heiniger, Rapho-Guillumette

The Matterhorn, which is between Italy and Switzerland, is said to be the most beautiful of all mountains.

Walker, Black Star

These are the rich wheat lands of Kansas.

## The Lowlands

In some parts of the world, there are lands that are almost flat. These flat lands are called plains. They may stretch for miles and miles and miles. On these fertile lands, wheat, cotton, corn, rice, or other crops are grown.

Cattle are raised on the cowboy flatlands of South America.

Ewing Galloway; Rapho-Guillumette; Gendreau

Rice is a crop grown on some of the flatlands of China.

The Netherlands, where the Dutch live, is so low and flat that walls are built to keep out the sea.

## Rivers, Valleys, and Canyons

In almost every part of the world, you will find valleys and rivers. You will also find some places where the rivers have cut deep into the earth. Such deep valleys with steep slopes are called canyons.

Union Pacific Railroad

This is the Grand Canyon, the mightiest canyon of them all. It is in Arizona and it is a mile deep.

Grover, Rapho-Guillumette

Water travelers on the Nile River in Egypt

Ewing Galloway

The beautiful valley of the Susquehanna River in Pennsylvania

## The Hot and Wet Lands

In many parts of the world, the weather is always hot. Heavy rains fall almost every day. Trees and other plants grow so fast and so thick that they form jungles. What do you think it would be like if you lived in the jungle?

A swampy rice field on the faraway island of Java in the Pacific Ocean.

This is a part of the thick jungle in Brazil.

Gendreau, Black Star

The Congo River flows through the heart of the hot African jungle.

Ewing Galloway
Travelers crossing the
Sahara in North Africa

## Hot and Dry Lands

Other parts of the world are hot and
dry. Such dry places are called deserts.
Little, if any, rain falls. What rain
does fall is quickly soaked up by the
thirsty sand or soil. Yet many people
live even in these hot and dry places.

The white sands of New Mexico

Fritz Henle, Monkmeyer

There are also big deserts
in China and in Australia.

73

## The Cold Lands

Far to the north and far to the south are the lands of year-round ice and snow. Summer comes for a short time only. The winters are long and dark. Daylight comes for only a short time each day.

This Eskimo of the Far North is hunting sea animals in his kayak. He is using his harpoon as a weapon. Notice the big glacier.

Does it look cold? It **is** cold, for this camp has been made on the ice in the Far South. American explorers lived in the tents for many months.

This speedy ship is crossing the Atlantic Ocean.

## Oceans, Lakes, and Swamps

Most of the earth's surface—almost three quarters of it—is covered with water. There are many lakes, seas, and mighty oceans. In them are found different kinds of animals and plants.

This is a balsa boat among the reeds of a big lake in South America.

Fairchild Aerial Surveys; Severin, Black Star; Borsig, Monkmeyer

And this is a swamp in Florida where many lovely trees and grasses grow.

## How Do We Know the Earth Is Round?

International

Long ago, people thought the earth was flat. But now we know that it is almost as round as a ball. Here is a picture of the earth taken from a rocket. You will notice that the shape of the earth is curved.

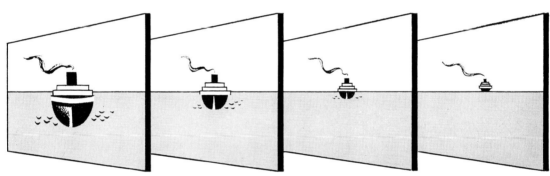

You can prove that the earth is round. If you live by the sea or by a very big lake, watch a ship as it goes out toward the sky line. It grows smaller and smaller as it gets farther away.

When the ship reaches the sky line, it begins to go out of sight. All at once, you find that the body of the ship has disappeared. You can see only the smokestacks. After a while, even the smokestacks can no longer be seen. All you can see is a little smoke rising into the sky. Watch long enough, and even that disappears.

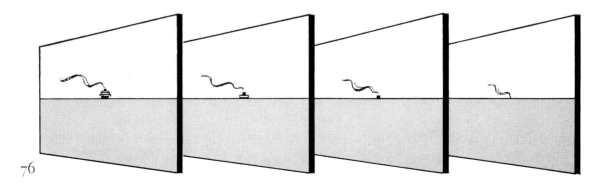

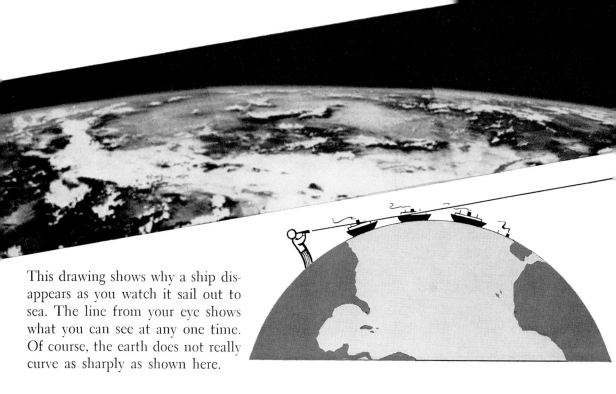

This drawing shows why a ship disappears as you watch it sail out to sea. The line from your eye shows what you can see at any one time. Of course, the earth does not really curve as sharply as shown here.

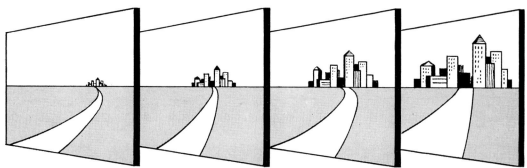

If you do not live by the sea or by a very large lake, you can still tell that the earth is round. When you are on a trip some time, if the land is flat, watch as you come toward a big city. When you are several miles away, you will begin to notice the tips of some high towers or church spires, and the tops of tall buildings. As you come nearer to the city, you see more and more of the buildings. If the whole earth were flat in shape, you would be able to see all parts of these buildings at once.

In the same way, as you drive toward mountains, you can see their tops long before you see the entire mountains.

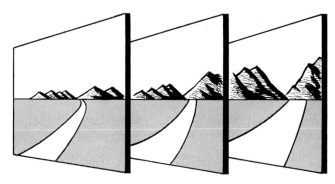

## What Makes Day and Night?

Have you ever watched the sun rise in the morning? Have you ever seen it go out of sight at night?

If so, it may be hard for you to believe that the sun does not travel across the sky. Perhaps, also, you think that the earth on which you live and play doesn't move at all. But it does. **The earth is moving all the time.**

Have you ever noticed how a top spins? The earth turns around in about the same way. It takes 24 hours to turn all the way around once.

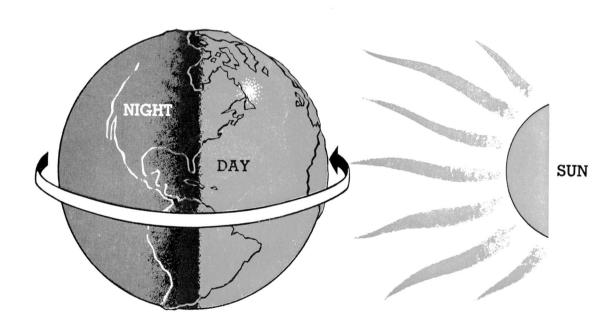

When the part of the earth on which we live faces the sun, we have daylight. When it is turned away from the sun, we have night.

## Make Your Own Day and Night

To make your own day and night, all you need is a table lamp, a small globe, and a dark room.

Put the globe and the lamp on a table or on the floor. Take the shade off the lamp and turn on the light. Turn off all other lights.

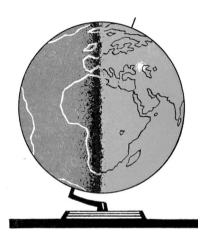

The light is your make-believe sun and the globe is the earth. Notice how one half of the globe is lighted. The other half is dark. It is daytime on the half of the earth which faces the light. It is nighttime on the other half.

Now have your father or mother help you to put a bit of soft clay on the place where you live. Keep the clay on the dark side of the globe. Then turn the globe slowly from left to right. That's how the real earth turns.

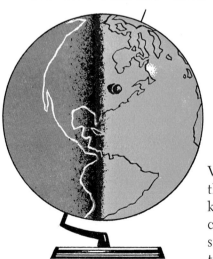

When the clay begins to come into the light, that is sunrise. As you keep turning the globe, the clay comes to the middle of the lighted side. It is now noon. As you continue to turn the globe, the clay leaves the light. That is sunset, and then it is night once more.

79

## The Earth Travels Around the Sun, Too

You have now learned that it is the earth which moves, and not the sun. You have also learned that the earth takes one full day of 24 hours to turn completely around once.

But that is not the only way in which the earth moves. While it is spinning, it is also moving almost in a circle around the sun.

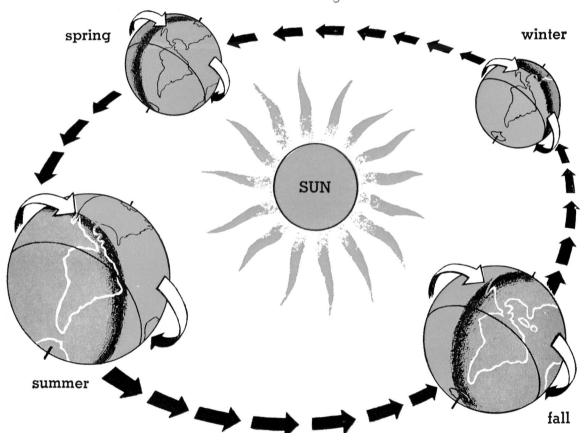

In traveling around the sun, the earth moves very fast, much faster than the fastest airplane. But it has to travel a long, long way. It takes the earth a whole year—or a few hours more than 365 days—to travel all the way around the sun.

During that time, you may skate in the winter. You see the flowers bloom in the spring. You paddle and swim in the summer. And you see the leaves drop off the trees in the fall.

## Why Do We Have Spring, Summer, Fall, and Winter?

In the summer, we have long hours of daylight. This makes the weather warm. In winter, the days are shorter and the weather is colder. In spring and fall, the hours of daylight and night are about the same. Then the weather is neither too hot nor too cold.

You can find out what makes the days long in the summer and short in winter with a globe for the earth and a lamp for the sun. Mark the place where you live on the globe with chalk. Darken the room and place your globe and the lamp as shown in the first picture. Be sure your globe is on a slant, as in the picture, because this is the way the real earth is tipped.

Now the globe of the earth is in its summer position. Turn the globe slowly to make day and night. Do you see that the place where you live is in the sunlight for a long time? So much sunlight makes the weather warm.

Now the globe has moved around the sun to its winter position. Turn the globe to make day and night. The place where you live is in the sunlight for a short time. It is in the dark, night side for a long time. The short winter days do not give us much heat, so winters are cold.

The people on the bottom part of the earth have their winter when we have summer. They have summer when we have winter. Do you see why?

## What Keeps the Earth Moving Around the Sun?

Tie the end of a string firmly around a rubber ball. Make believe that the ball is the earth and that your head is the sun. Swing the ball around your head as shown in the picture.

What keeps the ball swinging around your head? What would happen if you let the string go? It is the string that keeps the ball from flying away. It is the force of your arm which keeps the ball moving around your head.

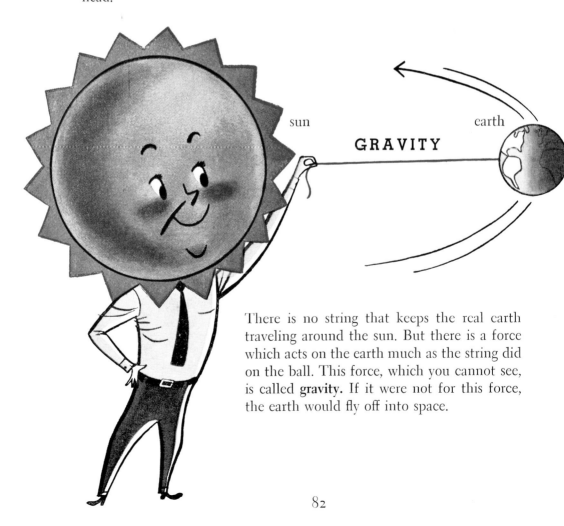

sun          GRAVITY          earth

There is no string that keeps the real earth traveling around the sun. But there is a force which acts on the earth much as the string did on the ball. This force, which you cannot see, is called **gravity.** If it were not for this force, the earth would fly off into space.

## What Makes Things Fall to the Earth?

The force of gravity pulls all things toward the earth.

Throw a ball into the air and it will fall back to earth.

Jump off a stool or a branch of a tree, and down you come.

ien Aigner

If you drop a sheet of paper, a rock, or a ball, they will all fall to earth.

There is an old saying that "Everything that goes up must come down." When an airplane runs out of gasoline, it, too, must land. Even birds, if they stop using their wings to keep them up, come back to earth.

If it were not for this pulling force, everything —people, balls, animals, and rocks—would go flying off into space.

# What Do You Mean When You Say "Up" or "Down"?

Look carefully at this drawing. It shows boys and girls who live in different parts of the world.

You will notice that "up" for each child is above his head. It is different for each boy and girl, like the spokes that come out from the center of a wagon wheel.

You will also notice that "down" means underneath for each boy and girl. The direction is the same here for each one. Down means in the direction of the center of the earth.

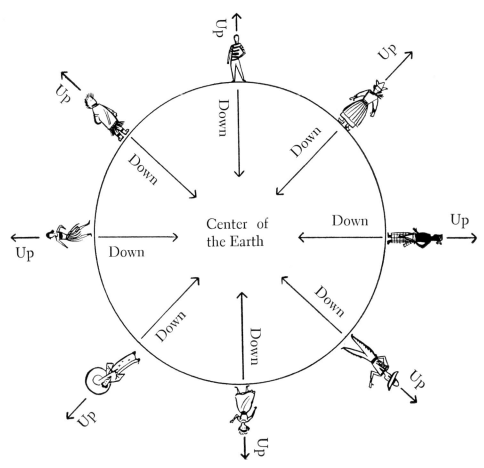

The force of gravity pulls everything toward the center of earth. It is this force which tells us which way is down. Up is the opposite of down.

## How to Find North During the Day

When people travel from place to place, they need to know the direction in which they are going if they are not to get lost. The pilot of an airplane must know his directions. So must the captain of a ship. And so must your father and mother when they go on a trip in the car.

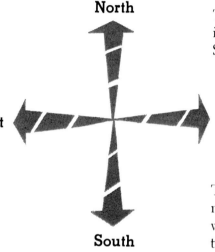

There are four main directions used by people in all parts of the world. They are North, South, East, and West.

The positions of the directions never change, no matter where you are, so, if you can tell where North is, you can always find the other three directions.

Here is how you can find North on a sunny day if you live on the top half of the world. Get an old broomstick, or any kind of stick. Set it up in the ground where the sun can shine on it at noon. At 12 o'clock noon (or 1 o'clock if you have daylight-saving time) look at the stick's shadow. The shadow points North. Lay another stick on the shadow so you can tell which way is North even when it is dark.

85

## Where Are South, East, and West?

Now stand behind the stick at noon. Look in the same direction that the stick's shadow is pointing. Like the stick's shadow, you, too, are facing **North.**

The direction behind you is **South.**

The direction on your left where the sun goes out of sight in the evening is **West.**

On your right is the direction where you first see the sun in the morning. That direction is **East.**

Ewing Galloway

Which direction does your front door face? your kitchen door?

Have you ever seen a weather vane something like this? It is used to tell the direction from which the wind is blowing. The letters N, S, E, and W stand for the words North, South, East, and West. The arrow turns around in the wind so that its point shows where the wind is blowing from. Where would it be blowing from if the arrow pointed to E? to W? to S?

## How Can We Find North at Night?

At night, if the sky is clear and the stars are out, go out and look at the sky. Look in the direction toward which the shadow of your broomstick pointed at noon. If you laid a stick on the shadow, you will know exactly which way to look.

Stand by your broomstick and look up into the sky at a point about halfway between the ground and overhead. There you will find a fairly bright star, the brightest star in that part of the sky. It is the North Star, which is always above the North Pole of the earth. It never changes its position in the sky. Once you know where the North Star is, you can find North at night, no matter where you are on the top half of the world. There is another way to find the North Star by using the Big Dipper, which you will find on page 148.

## What Else Do We Use to Find Our Way?

Now that you know directions, you can perhaps find your way by using a map. A map is a kind of picture showing where places are.

On this page is a picture of a map made by Frank. He made it of the small town where he lived. It shows the streets and some of the buildings he visits now and then.

Can you tell how you think Frank would go from his home . . .

to school

to the library

to the police station

to the store

to the park

to the swimming pool

to the fire station

to the railroad depot

Perhaps you will want to make your own map of the streets near your home. Ask your father, mother, or teacher to help you.

# How to Use a Road Map

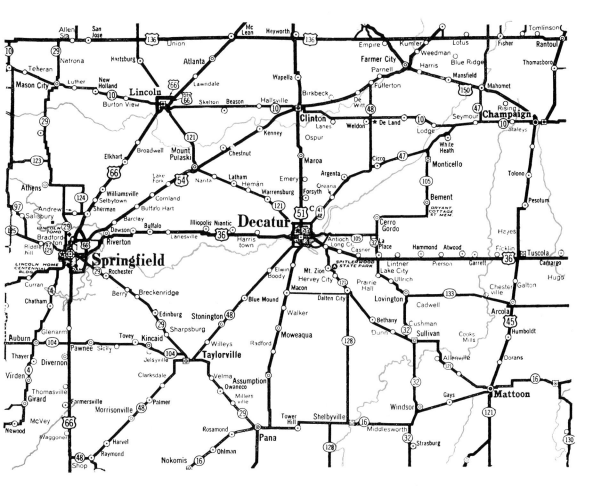

If you look at the map carefully, you will find the names of big and little places. You will also find roads marked on it. Each road has a number. Can you find such a road number?

Look for the name Springfield on the map. It is a town in Illinois where Lincoln once lived. Now look for Decatur. Which way would you go from Springfield to Decatur? What is the number of the road?

Now find Champaign on the map.

What road would you take to go from Decatur to Champaign?

# How Do Sailors and Airmen Find Their Way?

There are no roads or road signs in the air or on the ocean. How then do airplane pilots and sea captains find their way from one place to another?

They both use special maps. They also have an instrument with which they can tell the exact position of the sun by day and of the stars by night. Then they can tell from their maps exactly where they are.

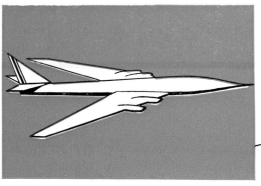

Radios and telephones also help them. Airplanes often follow radio beams. These are like roads in the sky which you cannot see.

Ewing Galloway; Airguide

Ships and airplanes also have an instrument that tells them the direction they are going. This instrument is called a compass. The needle on the compass always points to the North.

If you have a compass, ask your father how to tell direction with it. Take it out to the yard with you. See if the shadows cast by the stick in the ground and the pointer on your compass point in the same direction—North. Now turn around and face South. To what direction does the pointer point?

## The Earth Is Surrounded by a Blanket of Air

The earth we live on is covered with a blanket of air. It goes up for miles and miles above us.

We cannot see air, but it is all around us. It is this air that we breathe every minute, day and night, as long as we live. Without this air, we could not live. Without it, every animal and plant also would die very quickly.

Suzanne Szasz; Westveer, Black Star

The air makes it possible for clouds to float along in the sky. Without it, you could not fly your kite. Birds could not fly without air. Nor could airplanes.

The higher you go, the less air there is. On the top of a high mountain, there is much less air than in the valley below.

## How Do We Know Air Is Real?

If we cannot see air, and if it has no color, taste, or smell, then how do we know it is real?

Here is an empty glass. At least it looks empty. But is it really? Let's find out!

Take a piece of newspaper, crumple it, and put it into the glass. Press it to the bottom so it will not fall out when you turn the glass upside down.

Get a large bowl and fill it with water. Now hold the glass upside down and lower it slowly into the bowl of water, all the way to the bottom. Then take the glass out of the water. Be sure to keep it upside down. If you look at the paper, you will find that it is dry, even though the glass was all the way under water. Can you tell why?

The glass was full of something that kept the water out. It was full of air. When you put the glass in the water, the air kept the water from filling the glass and getting the paper wet.

# Air Has Weight, Too

If air is real, it should have weight, just as a ball, a stone, a top, or a doll has weight. Here is a way you can prove it has weight. All you need are two balloons, a stick, and some string.

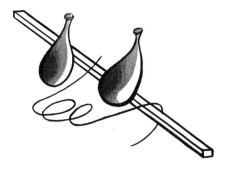

Blow two balloons full of air and tie them with string so the air cannot get out. Fasten one balloon to each end of your stick like this. Now fasten a string to the middle of the stick. Move it until the stick is level like this.

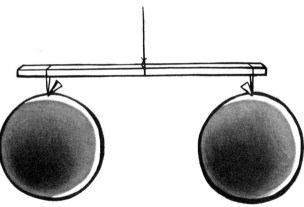

Let the air out of one balloon. What happens?

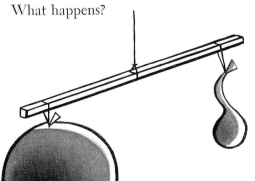

The balloon that has air in it pulls down one end of the stick. This proves that the balloon full of air is heavier than the empty balloon.

Air works for us in many ways. Wind, which is moving air, pushes against windmills and makes them work. This is a windmill in Holland. It is used to pump water.

This windmill, on an American farm, helps to make electricity for the farmer's house and barns.

Gendreau; Wincharger Corp.; Morris Rosenfeld, courtesy Ansco; Eastern Air Lines

Moving air pushes against the sails to make this boat go across the water.

Air, moving very fast over and under the wings, makes a moving airplane leave the ground and stay in the air.

Can you think of other ways that air works for us?

## Fun with Air

Did you ever make a pinwheel? Or a toy sailboat? Here is how you make a pinwheel.

Cut a sheet of heavy paper six inches wide and six inches long. Draw lines across from corner to corner to find the center. Cut in three inches along the lines from each corner.

Bend over every other corner so that they meet at the center. Push a straight pin through these corners at the center of the paper. Now fasten the pinwheel to a smooth stick or pencil. Bend the paper to make the pinwheel turn freely.

Blow on the pinwheel and watch it turn. Take it out into the yard and run into the wind with it.

You can make a simple sailboat like this out of scrap wood. The sail is just a piece of stiff paper. Put the boat in the bathtub when you are having a bath. Blow on it to make wind, and watch it sail along.

## Air on the Move

The air around us is always on the move. It is never at a standstill. It sometimes moves so slowly that you don't even know it is moving. At other times, it moves with great speed and force. It is then that we have storms, hurricanes, tornadoes, and waterspouts.

A hurricane whipping the trees on a tropical island in the Pacific.

A windy day in Chicago.

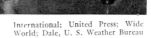

International; United Press; Wide World; Dale, U. S. Weather Bureau

A waterspout near the coast of Italy.

A tornado, or twister, whirls across the country.

# What Makes Air Move?

What makes the air move?    Why do we have winds?

Ask your mother to light a candle. After a while, hold your hand above the flame, high enough so you will not get burned. You will find that the air is warmer than it is at the side of the candle. When air is heated, it takes up more room. It also becomes lighter, so that the heavier cold air moves in and pushes it up.

Smoke rises from a bonfire as the warm air rises.

Open your refrigerator door. Hold your hand beneath, and you will feel the cold air falling toward the floor. It moves down, because it is heavier than the warm air in the room.

The sun heats some places on the earth more than other places. The air above these hot places gets warm. Colder air moves in to take its place. This moving air is called wind.

## What Makes Our Weather?

Weather is very important, for it affects almost everything we do. It may be hot or cold, wet or dry, calm or windy.

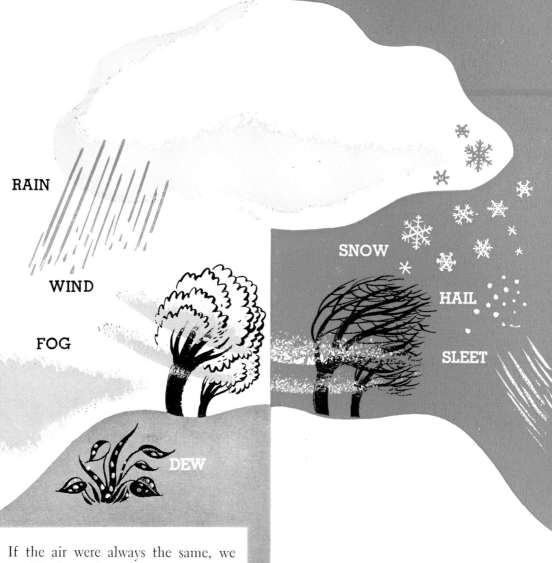

RAIN

WIND

FOG

DEW

SNOW

HAIL

SLEET

If the air were always the same, we would always have the same kind of weather. But air is never the same. It is always changing. It is these changes in moving air which bring us our weather. Heat, cold, and water cause some of these changes.

Different kinds of air bring some of the things shown in this drawing. Rain, snow, fog, dew, hail, and sleet are all made from water which gets into the air and comes down again.

## How Does Water Get Into the Air?

Put a little water in a dish. Then set it on a window sill where the sun can shine on it. Leave it for several days. What happens to the water?

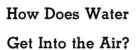

What happens to rain puddles on the street when the sun comes out again? Where does the water go?

Gendreau

Ask your mother to heat some water in a pan until it gets very hot. What happens? Can you see anything rising into the air? What is it?

You can see from these experiments that water turns into steam, or vapor. It rises into the air from puddles, ponds, rivers, lakes, and oceans.

99

## Cloud Shapes in the Sky

Have you ever looked at the clouds in the sky? Perhaps you have seen lion, cat, sheep, and other animal shapes there! Where did these clouds come from? What are they made of?

On a cold wintry day, perhaps you have noticed that you can see your breath come out in the form of a tiny cloud. The air you breathe out is warm, and full of water vapor from your lungs. When this warm, damp air hits the cold air outside, it is quickly cooled. The water vapor turns into tiny drops of water and makes a small cloud.

The cloud shapes you see floating in the air are made in the same way. When vapor rises from lakes, rivers, and oceans, it is cooled higher up. The water vapor turns into tiny drops of water to form clouds.

# What Makes It Rain?

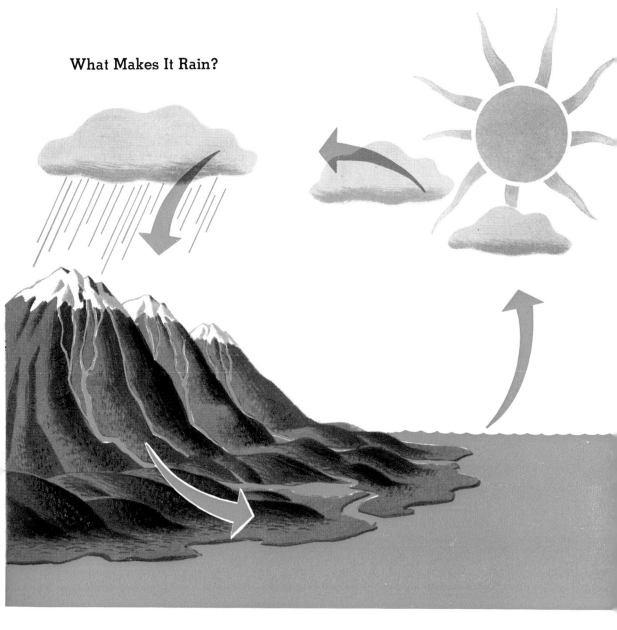

Water vapor rises into the air from ponds, rivers, lakes, and oceans. You cannot see the water vapor until the air with the water vapor in it is cooled, when clouds are formed.

These clouds move along with the moving air. Sometimes they are pushed higher into colder air. When this happens, the tiny water drops become bigger and heavier. When they are too heavy to float, the water drops fall to the earth. When this happens, we know that it is raining.

## Make Your Own Rain

Ask your mother to put a pan of water on the stove until it gets hot.

When it begins to steam, get a pitcher and put some ice cubes in it. Hold this in the steam, or vapor cloud, which is rising from the pan.

The vapor cloud which rises from the pan is the same as the vapor of which clouds are made.

The vapor is hot and the pitcher is cold. When the vapor clouds reach the pitcher, they turn into drops of water. These cling to the pitcher for a while. But as more and more drops of water form, they fall back into the pan of hot water.

Look at the picture on the last page again. You will then see that the rain you have made indoors is made in much the same way that rain is made outdoors.

## Snow

If it didn't snow, you could not make a snowman, go sledding, or have snowball fun! But what is snow? How is it made? Where did it come from and where does it go?

Ewing Galloway; Zelenka, Black Star

The air is much colder in winter than in summer. When the tiny drops of water vapor in the clouds become big and heavy and it is very cold, they turn into snowflakes. The sky is full of soft, feathery snowflakes instead of falling raindrops.

If you look at snowflakes through a magnifying glass, you will be surprised to find that each snowflake has six points. But no one has ever found two snowflakes that are exactly alike. When the snow melts, it becomes water once more.

103

## Hail and Sleet

Have you ever been out in a hailstorm? If you have, you will know that hailstones are often as large as small marbles. Sometimes, they may be as big as small plums or lemons. What makes hail?

Sometimes, when raindrops fall, strong winds blow them straight up again into colder air. The raindrops freeze and fall toward the earth again. As they fall, they are covered with more water, which is also frozen. As they go up and down in this way, they grow bigger and bigger.

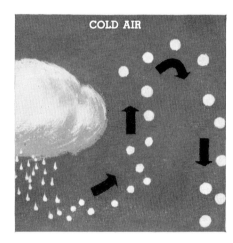

United Press; Cole, Monkmeyer

When they grow too big to be carried up any more, they drop to the earth.

Sleet is frozen or partly frozen rain. It covers trees and bushes and telephone wires and everything else to make a fairyland like this. Sleet is made when rain freezes or partly freezes.

## Make Your Own Dew and Frost

Have you gone out one morning and found grass, flowers, and spiderwebs covered with dew? Where did it come from? Let's find out.

Put some ice cubes in a glass. Fill the glass with water. In just a short while, drops of water will form on the outside of the glass. This usually works better in summer than in winter. It also works better if there is plenty of water in the air.

Because of the ice cubes, the glass of water is cold. The outside air is warm. When this warm air touches the cold glass, the water vapor in the air turns into drops of water on the outside of the glass.

In winter, you may wake up on a cold morning and see frost on your windowpanes. What has happened? It is cold outside and warm inside. The moisture in the air inside comes in touch with the cold window. There it turns into water and is frozen into pretty designs.

On a cold day, blow on a windowpane and see what happens.

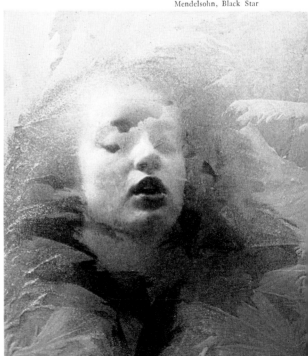

## What Makes Thunder and Lightning?

Now and then, the sky looks black and angry with heavy clouds. Suddenly there is a bright flash of light. In a few seconds, the flash of light is followed by a loud clap of thunder. The flashes of light are brighter and the crash of the thunder is louder than the best fireworks display could be.

Thunder is just a big noise. It may startle you, but it can't hurt anyone.

You can make your own small thunder if you want to. Just blow an empty paper bag full of air. After you have blown the bag as full of air as possible, hold the neck of the bag tightly so the air cannot escape.

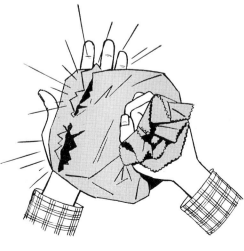

Now hit the bag hard with your other hand. It will break with a loud bang. That is all thunder is. It is just air making a loud noise.

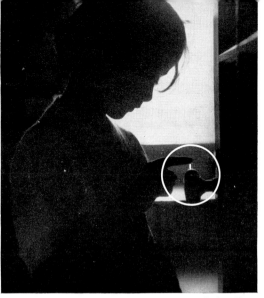

Lucien Aigner

The flash of light you see before you hear the rumble of thunder is lightning. It is this lightning which makes it thunder.

Before we find out how, let's try an experiment! It will work best on a cold winter day. Shuffle across any rug you may have in your house. Then bring your finger very close to a metal doorknob. A spark will jump from your finger to the knob. The spark is small, but it is really just like real lightning.

Carew, Monkmeyer

Lightning is just a big spark of electricity that jumps from cloud to cloud or from a cloud to the earth. This lightning heats the air and pushes it apart. Then the air rushes together again with a big bang. So we have a lightning flash, followed by a thunderclap.

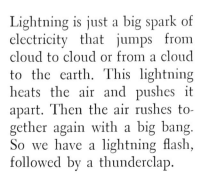

Wind 20 miles an hour

city 1 ——————————— 20 miles ——————————— city 2

## What Does the Weatherman Do?

Suppose that you live in city 2 and you have a friend in city 1. Your friend calls you up and tells you it is raining hard where he lives. He says that there is a wind blowing 20 miles an hour toward your city. If you remember that wind brings changes in weather, you can tell that the rain is coming in your direction. It will reach your city in about an hour, unless the wind changes its direction or something else happens.

This is the way the weatherman works. He gets reports about the weather from all parts of the country. And he has many instruments to help him tell what changes to expect from the weather. They tell him which way the wind is blowing, how hot it is, how wet the air is, and many other things. These all help him to tell what kind of weather to expect.

It is a good thing we have weathermen. The kind of weather we are going to have is important to the farmer and airman, to ships at sea, and to many others. The weatherman is not always right, for the winds may change and other things may happen to change the weather from what he expected. But he is right a good part of the time.

U. S. Weather Bureau

# How You Can Tell How Hot or How Cold It Is

This is a thermometer. It is one of the most important tools the weatherman uses. It tells us how hot or how cold the air is. The liquid in the thin glass tube rises when the air gets warm. It falls when the air cools.

As you can see, there are marks on the thermometer. Look carefully, and you will find 0, 10, 20, 30, 40, and so on. Also look between these figures, such as between the figures 40 and 50. You will find 5 little spaces. Each of these spaces means 2 degrees.

On this thermometer, the liquid is level with the 50 mark. That means the temperature is 50°.

**freezing point**

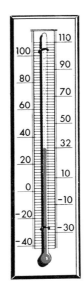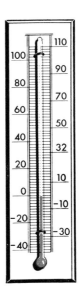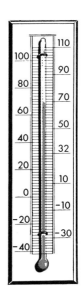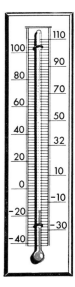

If the liquid falls to 32°, water will freeze and it will be time to get out your skates. If it falls to 0, that is zero. When the liquid falls below 0, we say the temperature is below zero and we count downward.

If the liquid is up to the mark 70, how hot is it? If it falls exactly halfway between −10 and −20, how cold is it?

## Keep Your Own Weather Records

You can have fun keeping your own record of the weather.

First you will need a thermometer. Fasten it on the outside of a window on the north side of the house. You should be able to read it from the inside.

You will also need a weather vane like this one. Perhaps your father will help you make one. Fasten it to a pole outside the house. Remember that the arrow will always point in the direction the wind comes from. If the arrow points to the W, that means the wind is blowing from the west.

Each day you will want to know

1. How hot or cold it is

2. Where the wind is blowing from

3. What the sky looks like—clear, cloudy, or partly cloudy

4. If there is rain, snow, or fog

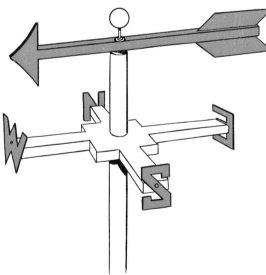

Look outside, look up at the sky, and look at your thermometer and weather vane.

## A Weather Calendar

Make a chart like this on a large sheet of paper. Each square stands for one day. Put the number 1 in the bottom right-hand corner of the square of the day on which the month begins. If the first day of the month is Tuesday, put the 1 in the square under the word Tuesday. If the first day of the month is Friday or any other day, put the 1 in the square under the name of that day. Then put numbers in the other squares as shown here. Work from left to right.

| Name of month |  |  |  |  |  |  |
|---|---|---|---|---|---|---|
| SUN | MON | TUES | WED | THURS | FRI | SAT |
|  |  | 1 | 2 | 3 | 4 | 5 |
| 6 | 7 | 8 | 9 | 10 | 11 | 12 |
| 13 | 14 | 15 | 16 | 17 | 18 | 19 |
| 20 | 21 | 22 | 23 | 24 | 25 | 26 |
| 27 | 28 | 29 | 30 |  |  |  |

**snow**

**sunny**

**fog**

**rainy**

**cloudy**

**partly cloudy**

In the top left corner of each square you make a small picture to tell if the day is sunny, rainy, cloudy, or partly cloudy.

In the bottom left corner, you put the letter N, S, E, or W to show the direction from which the wind is blowing. Put your thermometer reading in the top right corner.

A square for one day might look like this

Another square might look like this

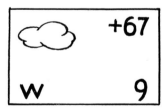

or this

What does this picture say?

It says that on the fourth day of the month, it was sunny. The wind was from the west and the temperature was 70.

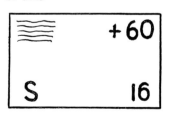

111

## What Happens to the Rain After It Falls?

You may not like it if it rains when you have planned to go on a picnic. But if we didn't have any rain, no plants would grow. Without plants, no animals could live. And without plants and animals, **we** couldn't live.

Gendreau: H. Armstrong Roberts

When it rains, much of the water sinks into the ground. It is this water and the light of the sun which help to make the grass and all plants green. Some of the water goes back into the air in the form of water vapor. Some of the water runs into brooks, streams, lakes, and oceans.

In the Far North and Far South, snow never melts. There you will find huge snow and ice fields. You will also find snow all the year around on the highest mountains.

In big cities like Rochester, N. Y., you may see huge water reservoirs like this.

Lucien Aigner; Cushing

## Where Does the Water We Use Come From?

In some places, water is pumped from lakes, from rivers, or from under the ground. The pumps raise the water into tanks or reservoirs. The water is made clean and safe for us to drink before it runs through pipes to our homes.

Water tanks like this may be seen in small towns.

This is a type of well you may see at a farm in the country.

Wendnagel and Co.; United Press

This is a pumping station which pumps water from Lake Michigan for the use of people living in Chicago.

## Water Works for Us

You have already learned how air works for us. Water works for us, too, in many ways. We couldn't bathe without it, or wash dishes, or even live. Many factories would have to stop working because they couldn't do their work without using water.

This is a mighty dam where the water is used to make electricity.

Running water makes this wheel go around. The wheel makes other machinery go. This, in turn, can be used to grind grain, to saw wood, and to do other work.

This ore ship is passing through the Soo Canal on its way from Lake Huron to Lake Superior.

In what ways besides these shown on this page do we use water?

Bureau of Reclamation; Soil Conservation Service; Gendreau

In many places, rich soil covers the earth.

## What Is the Earth Made of?

Deep down in the earth we are told it is very hot because it is made up of hot, melted rock. We know more about the surface of the earth because we live on it. It is made of soil, rock, and gravel.

Other parts of the earth's surface are covered with sand.

You will find rocks like these along the shore, among the mountains, and in many other places. Everywhere underneath the soil, sand, and even the oceans, there is solid rock.

115

## A Mountain
## That Breathes Fire and Smoke

The solid rock on the surface of the earth is something like the crust on a pie. Deep down under this rock crust is melted rock, something like thick, hot juice. The mountains on the earth were formed when the earth cooled. Forces inside the earth squeezed and bent layers of rock into mountains and mountain ranges.

On this page, you see a picture of a volcano in action. White-hot, melted rock is squirting out from beneath the earth's surface. Flames and smoke sometimes belch out of the mountain.

Ewing Galloway

This volcano started in a cornfield in Mexico. It slowly grew bigger and bigger until it is now a high mountain. The melted rock which flows down the mountain side is called lava. As it cools, it becomes solid rock.

Here is what a volcano would probably look like if you could see inside it. You can see that the melted rock comes to the surface through a long tubelike opening.

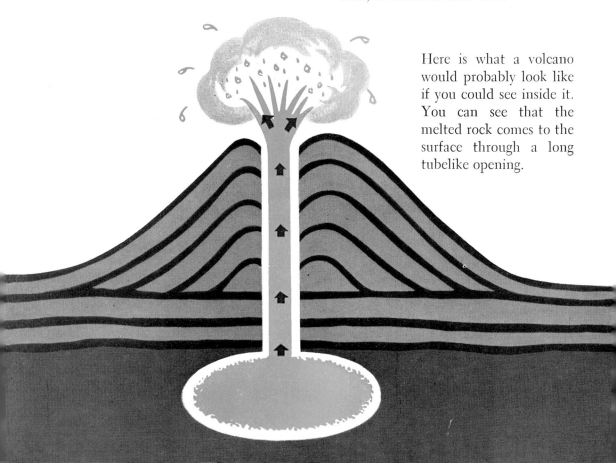

If you have been in Yellowstone Park, perhaps you have seen this spout of water shoot into the air now and again. It is Old Faithful, the most famous geyser in the world. About once every hour regularly, a high column of water and steam shoots into the air.

If you could see inside a geyser, this is what you would see. Water deep down in the tube gets boiling hot from the hot rocks around it. As the water gets boiling hot, it turns into steam. There is no way for the steam to escape. So, when there is enough steam, it blows up the water ahead of it in the form of a high spout.

## A Giant Water Pistol

117

## Water Changes the Surface of the Earth

Water has had much to do with the way the earth looks today. Running water can be both harmful and helpful to man.

Running water can wear away rocks to make beautiful scenery like this.

Or it can cut away good soil and ruin farm lands.

Running water sometimes digs deep canyons like the Grand Canyon. At other times, it makes wide, open valleys such as this, where the soil is rich and farm crops can be grown.

You can see for yourself how water wears things away. Make a little hill of garden soil or sand. Turn the garden hose on it. Do you see how the water carries the soil or sand away?

Union Pacific Railroad; Ewing Galloway; Gendreau

# Wind and Ice Change the Earth's Surface

When water freezes, it takes up more room. Milk does, too. Did you ever take in the milk bottle on a cold winter morning and have it look like this?

Water in tiny cracks in the rocks freezes. As it freezes, it gets bigger. From year to year, the cracks get bigger and this helps to break up the rocks.

Wind and water changed these rocks after a long period of time to form this bridge.

A glacier is a slowly moving mass of ice which scrapes and scours the surface of the earth. When it melts, it leaves soil and huge rocks on the surface of the earth.

Union Pacific Railroad

This is a part of Bryce Canyon National Park in Utah. Wind, sand, and water wore away the rock to make beautiful shapes.

U. S. Geological Survey,
Union Pacific Railroad

119

## Man, too, Has Changed the Earth's Surface

He plowed the vast prairie lands. There, today, great crops of wheat and corn are grown.

The earth we live on is ours to use and to enjoy. We should use it wisely if we want to keep it a beautiful and happy place in which to live.

The surface of our own land does not look the same today as it did when it was first settled. What man has done since that time has changed it a great deal. Sometimes, he made changes that were good.

By bringing water through pipes or canals, he has turned much desert land into good farm land.

Sometimes man's work has not been good. He has cut down trees from hillsides. These trees kept water from washing soil away.

He has often been careless in causing forest fires. When this happens, birds, deer, and other animals are killed or left homeless.

Can you think of some ways in which we can protect soil, forests, and places of natural beauty?

120

## How Soil Is Made

Water, sunlight, air, and heat are all important to us. But, without soil, we could not grow plants. And if there were no plants, we would have no animals. Without plants and animals, we would have no food.

Long, long ago there were only rocks on the earth. These rocks were slowly broken up into small pieces because of wind, ice, heat, cold, and water. Later, as plants grew and died, they became a part of the soil. This first soil was not nearly so good as the soil we have today.

## You Can Make Your Own Soil

First, get some fine sand. Then dry some clay and crush it into powder. Mix it with the sand. Find some dried leaves and crumble them. Mix this leaf powder with the sand and clay. Now add some water and you will have a sort of soil. Put it in a flowerpot and grow some seeds in it.

It takes a long, long time for good soil to form. That is why we should protect the soil on our land.

sand

clay

soil

leaves

121

## How Soil Works for Us

The good soil on the surface of the earth is never very deep. There are only about six inches of it. Without this fine topsoil, we could not have what is shown on this page.

The topsoil must be soft and crumbly if seeds are to sprout and grow up into the light. When topsoil is soft, there are air spaces so the roots can get air. It holds water for the thirsty roots, too. And it has minerals that the plants must have if they are to grow well.

Lanks, Black Star

Orange trees and all other fruit trees will only grow well in good soil.

The grass growing out of the soil feeds these cattle, as well as sheep and other animals.

Cotton, such as this, grows best in deep rich soil.

Gendreau; Sears, Black Star

## How Do We Use Sand and Clay?

Sand and clay come from rock. We use them in many ways to make other things.

Sand is used to help make glass.

Cement and sand and gravel are mixed together to make concrete.

Portland Cement Assoc.

Many bricks and tile and dinner dishes are made from clay.

Mortar for plastering is made with sand and lime.

Have you ever played with sand or modeled with clay? What other uses are made of these products?

## What Are Rocks Good For?

Maybe you think rocks are only good for throwing into water. But rocks are used in many other ways. This picture shows a quarry where stone is mined and shaped to make the walls of buildings. Some stone is crushed to make gravel for roads and for making cement.

Ewing Galloway

buildings

sidewalks

Here are pictures of how rocks are used. Can you think of other uses?

driveways

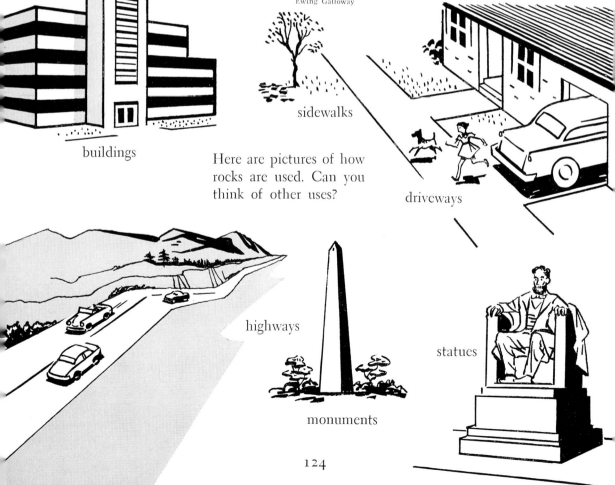

highways

monuments

statues

124

## Collecting Stones

Collecting is fun. Perhaps you already have a stamp collection, or an insect, match-cover, or shell collection.

Collecting rocks is one of the most interesting of hobbies. You will find rocks almost everywhere.

A good way to start is to pick up those you think are pretty in color. Stones which have been broken or polished into interesting shapes are also fun to collect.

Stones make good souvenirs of interesting places that you visit. Many persons think they are better than souvenir post cards.

125

## What We Get from the Earth

We get many, many valuable minerals from the earth besides soil and rocks and sand and clay. From these we make thousands of things we need and use.

Oil is found in pools deep in the ground. Wells are dug and the precious liquid is pumped to the surface.

This is an iron mine in Minnesota. The iron is found in a rock which is mined by big digger machines.

Ewing Galloway;
Bureau of Mines

Coal comes from the earth, too. Men dig into the earth and bring the coal to the surface.

126

Deep down in the earth, gas is found above oil pools. This is pumped out and used for cooking your food. Much of it is also used for heating homes.

This salt mine is in Grand Saline, Texas. The rock salt is brought to the surface, and then made pure for us to use.

Transcontinental Gas;
Morton Salt Co.; Cushing

The largest copper mine of its kind in the world is in Utah. From this pit we get copper ore which is used for making copper.

## More Minerals
## We Get
## from the Earth

This lead mine is in Missouri. Lead is an important metal used for making water pipes, bullets, paint, and other things.

Tin is also mined from such mines as this in a country in South America. It is used for coating tin cans and for many, many other things.

Nickel is a silvery-white metal which is very hard. This nickel mine is in Canada. Nickel does not rust. It is often mixed with iron to keep rust away.

128

Gold is mined in South Dakota and in other parts of the world. It is used for money, jewelry, fillings for teeth, and in other ways.

Silver is also a precious metal used for money, jewelry, and other things. This mine is in Colorado. Silver is mined in many other parts of the world.

This diamond mine is in South Africa. Diamond is the hardest of all substances. It is used for jewelry, but it is also used for cutting and grinding.

129

## What the Earth We Live on Means to Us

What a wonderful place this earth of ours is! Think of all the things we take for granted— the air we breathe; the heat and light of the sun; rain, sunshine, soil, and plants and animals! Yet no living thing could continue to live without these.

Mountains, plains, rivers, caves, canyons, forests, lakes, and waterfalls! In the midst of all these and other scenic wonders, men and all living things find shelter, clothing, and food.

Hibbs; Pickow, Three Lions

From beneath the surface of the earth, we get minerals and other treasures. Some of these help to heat our homes and to drive our cars. Others furnish us with the materials which our factories use to make all kinds of machines and goods.

Other people have used these treasures before we used them. Still others will continue to use them in the future. It is our duty to preserve and protect the world around us so that others may enjoy it, too.

# THE SKY ABOVE US

Cushing

131

Looking at the sky above us makes us think about a number of things. You may wonder why the sky is blue, what makes a rainbow, why the stars seem to twinkle, and where the stars go in the daytime.

You may want to know what the sun is made of and how hot it is. You may be puzzled, perhaps, because you don't always see a moon in the night sky. You may even wonder why you can sometimes see the moon by day—and why its shape changes from time to time.

From time to time, too, you see the sun and clouds turn into beautiful colors of red, orange, and yellow at sunrise and sunset. And you may wonder why.

In the following pages, you will learn many things as you explore the skies. You will even learn that shooting stars aren't really stars at all, and that some bright objects in the sky which look like stars are not really stars.

You will learn, too, how fast a space ship would have to travel if it were to leave the earth on a trip to the moon.

# What Can You See in the Daytime Sky?

You may see a beautiful sunset

Hoit, Cushing

. . . a sky full of fluffy clouds

Cushing; Myslis

. . . dark rain clouds with the rain pouring down

. . . a beautiful rainbow

. . . or birds and airplanes flying in the sky.

Szecsi, Black Star; Ewing Galloway

133

## What Can You See
## in the Sky at Night?

On clear nights, you may see a sky full of stars

or a bright silvery moon.

You may see what is called a shooting star.

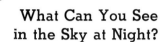

You may even see a bright evening star. It looks something
like this when you look at it
through a big instrument,
called a telescope.

Yerkes Observatory; Cushing

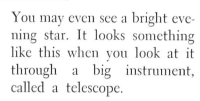

## How High Is the Sky?

There are really two kinds of sky. One is the blue sky made of air. It goes up only a few hundred miles. This is the sky of clouds, rainbows, and rain. Birds and airplanes fly through the lower part of this sky of air.

The other sky is where the sun, moon, and stars are. It is called space, and there is no air there. Space goes on and on so far that no one knows if it has an end.

## What Makes the Sky Blue?

When we look at the blue sky above us, we are really looking at air which is all lighted up by the sun.

Sunlight is made up of all the colors of the rainbow mixed together to make white light.

As sunlight comes into the air, it is spread out in all directions. The air also acts as a sort of sifter. It holds back the bluish colors of the sunlight more than the others. This is what makes the air seem blue.

Of course the sky is not always blue. Sometimes clouds hide so much sunlight that the sky is dark and gray.

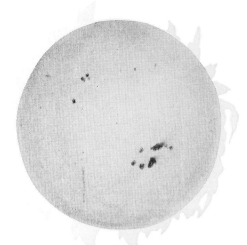

# The Brightest Object in the Sky

Mt. Wilson and Palomar Observatories

Huge tongues of fiery gas leap up for many thousands of miles above the sun's surface.

Our sun is really a star. It is the brightest object in the entire sky. It is a great ball of swirling, glowing gases that are far hotter than any fire could be.

But the sun is so far away that its heat is just right for us on the earth. Nothing could live on the earth if it were not for the sun's light and heat. Plants could not make food. Everything would be frozen solid. All living things depend upon the sun.

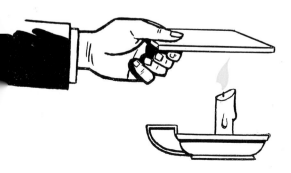

Never look at the sun with your bare eyes. It can injure them. If you want to see what the sun looks like, have your father hold a piece of glass over a candle flame so that it is heavily covered with black soot. Then look at the sun through this, or you can look through an old camera film.

## How Big Is the Sun?
## How Far Away Is It?

Our sun is very much like all the thousands of stars you see shining in the night sky. But it is so much nearer to us than the other stars that it looks much bigger and brighter.

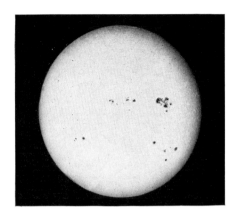

Our sun is just a middle-sized star. Even so, it is more than a million times bigger than the earth. If this glass bowl were the same size as the sun, more than a million "earth balls" the size of these marbles could be put inside it.

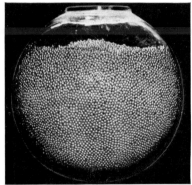

American Museum of Natural
History; Ufa from Penguin

The sun is 93 million miles away. To see how far that is, let us suppose that it were possible for us to go to the sun in a rocket space ship. Suppose that our space ship traveled seven miles in a second. At that speed we could go around the earth in just one hour! But it would take us five months, at that speed, to get to the sun! Of course, no one would ever want to go there, for the sun is so hot that it would burn us up long before we could reach it.

# What Makes a Rainbow?

The light we get from the sun is really made up of all the colors you see in a rainbow. Usually, these colors are all mixed up, and together they make white light. Now and then, these colors are separated. Then we have a rainbow. What happens to make a rainbow?

Maybe you have noticed that a rainbow usually comes during, or right after, a shower of rain. And the sun is always shining! When the sunlight hits the raindrops, the mixed-up colors are separated.

It is the drops that send the colors into your eyes. They send out orange, yellow, green, blue, and the other colors of the rainbow. Millions of raindrops work together and separate the white sunlight to make the beautiful rainbow with all its colors.

## Make Your Own Rainbow

You can easily make your own rainbow. Turn on the garden hose when the sun is shining. Turn the nozzle until you have a fine spray of water. Stand with your back to the sun and look at the spray. Do you see the rainbow you have made?

You can make a rainbow in another way, too. Place a small pocketbook mirror in a glass and fill the glass with water. The mirror should be on a slant, as shown in the picture. Place the glass where the sun can shine on the mirror. If you look around, you will find colors on the wall or ceiling. If you cannot see them, turn the glass a bit until you do.

## Clouds in the Sky

The sky is often full of clouds. Clouds have many different shapes. But they are all made up of tiny drops of water or ice. There are four main kinds of clouds that you see in the sky.

Ewing Galloway; U. S. Weather Bureau

On a summer day, you have probably seen clouds like these. They are little puffs of snowy white that look like fluffy cotton. They are called cumulus clouds. Little cumulus clouds, like these, are seen during good weather.

Sometimes you will see cumulus clouds that have piled up so much that they look like beautiful mountains high up in the sky. These are sometimes called thunderheads.

## These Clouds Bring Rain

On a dark, stormy day, rain clouds fill the sky. They come in many shapes and forms. Sometimes the sky is completely covered with them, as in this picture. Rain clouds are gray and dark, because they are so full of water that it is difficult for the light from the sun to get through.

Sometimes you can see a rainstorm coming. Did you ever see a big wall of clouds, like this, moving toward you? These are rain clouds, too. When they are directly overhead the wind will blow hard and it will probably rain heavily.

## Clouds That Look Like Sheets

Sometimes you can see long, thin sheets of clouds stretched across the sky. These are called stratus clouds. Stratus means sheetlike.

Sometimes clouds of this kind hang low in the sky. These are the clouds that make some of our winter days gray and dark. Rain or snow often comes from them.

Most clouds are made of tiny drops of water. But some clouds are formed so high in the sky that the water is frozen into tiny crystals of ice. This kind of thin, wispy cloud is an ice cloud.

Ewing Galloway; U. S.
Weather Bureau

143

## Do Stars Really Twinkle?

What is more beautiful than a night sky that is full of stars! What are stars? Like the sun, they are huge, hot balls of gas that are glowing brightly. But they are so far away that they look like tiny points of light twinkling in the sky.

This isn't a cloud! Each tiny speck of light is a giant star, or sun.

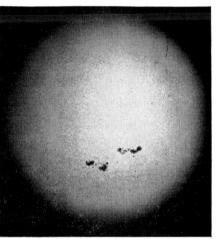

Yerkes Observatory; Mt. Wilson and Palomar Observatories

Real stars seem to twinkle in the sky. They look as if they have points. But they are really round like the sun. If you wanted to draw a real star, it would look like this.

When we draw stars, we usually make them with five points like this. It is this kind of star which you will find in the Stars and Stripes, the Flag of the United States.

Sometimes stars, like the Star of David, are made with six points like this. Badges worn by policemen in some cities also have six points.

144

## Why Do the Stars Look so Small?

This picture shows you why stars look like tiny points of light, although many of them are hundreds of times bigger than our sun. Notice how the nearest light shows up large and round. Notice how the other lights in the distance seem to become smaller and smaller. Yet you know that they are all the same size.

Stars are all different in size. But, except for our sun, they are all so far away that they look like tiny points of light.

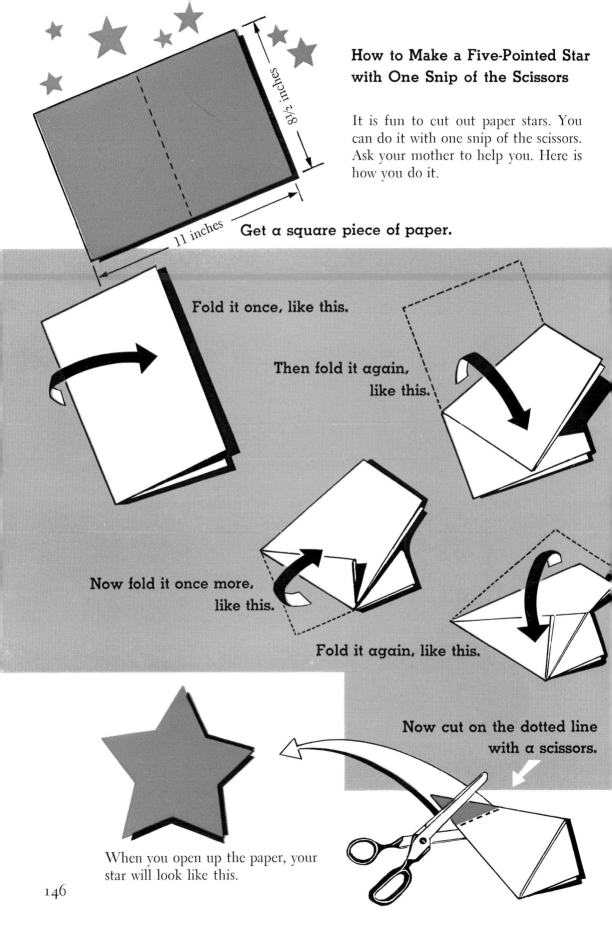

## How to Make a Five-Pointed Star with One Snip of the Scissors

It is fun to cut out paper stars. You can do it with one snip of the scissors. Ask your mother to help you. Here is how you do it.

8½ inches

11 inches

**Get a square piece of paper.**

**Fold it once, like this.**

**Then fold it again, like this.**

**Now fold it once more, like this.**

**Fold it again, like this.**

**Now cut on the dotted line with a scissors.**

When you open up the paper, your star will look like this.

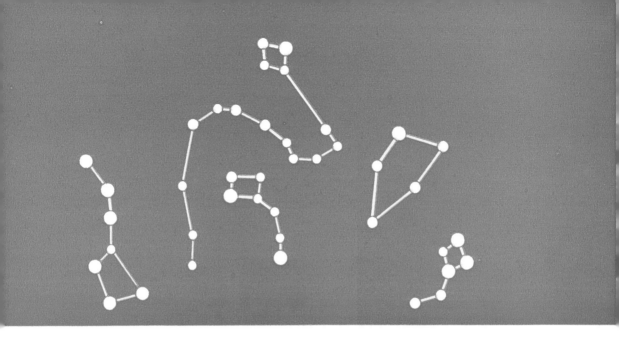

## Star Pictures in the Sky

When you look up into the sky on a clear night, you can see many, many stars. They seem to be all mixed up together. But if you look long enough, you may see interesting star pictures in the night sky. This is the way the Northern sky might look on a clear night. Can you find any star pictures?

Here is the same view of the sky as above. The thin lines are put into the drawing to show you some of the star pictures that you can see in the Northern sky on a clear night.

## The Big Dipper

Star pictures in the sky are simply groups of stars. Long, long ago, people looked up at the sky and imagined that these groups of stars looked like people, animals, or other objects. They named the star groups after the things they thought they looked like. Some of the star groups look like the things they are named after, but others do not.

The most important star group in the Northern sky is called the Big Dipper. It really looks something like a big dipper.

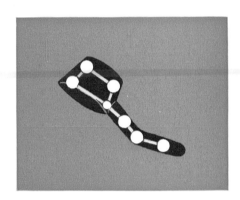

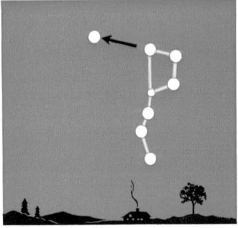

The Big Dipper is important because it helps us to find the North Star. The two end stars in the bowl of the dipper are called the "Pointers" because they point to the North Star, as shown in this picture.

The Big Dipper is not always in the same position. It goes around the North Star once every day. It also changes its position with the seasons. This picture shows how the Big Dipper looks right after dark in spring, summer, autumn, and winter.

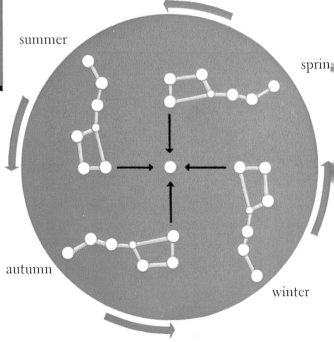

summer

sprin

autumn

winter

## Star Pictures and Their Stories

Another star picture you can see in the night sky is that of the Big and Little Bears.

The Big Bear is made up of the stars which form the Big Dipper and of other stars which are near it. The Little Bear is sometimes called the Little Dipper. It is part of the star group to which the North Star belongs. This picture shows how people imagine the Big Bear and the Little Bear look.

The story is told that once upon a time, there was a wicked old woman who had a son who was also very mean. They were punished for their wickedness by being changed into bears. Then the bears were grabbed by their short tails and swung round and round until they sailed far up into the sky where they kept swinging round and round the North Star. They were swung so hard that their tails stretched and stretched, and became very long. If you look at them, up in the sky, you will see how long their tails became. Of course, this is a make-believe story, just as the bears themselves are.

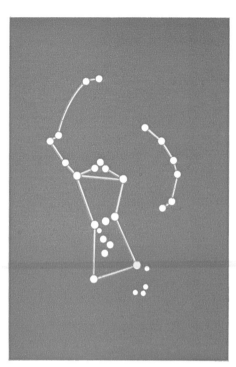

## Orion, the Mighty Hunter

If you will go out on a winter night and look up at the Southern sky, you will see a group of stars that looks like this. It is called Orion, the mighty hunter. Of course, there aren't any real lines up in the sky. They are put into this picture to help you see the stars that make up the picture of Orion.

This is the same group of stars, but now the picture of Orion has been drawn around the stars as people imagine they see him in the sky.

There are several stories about how Orion got up in the sky. One of the oldest stories is that Orion was a mighty hunter. No one in all the world could hunt as well as he. But Orion began to boast about how good he was. Boasting is never a good thing to do and Orion was finally punished for his boasting. One day, as he was hunting in the woods, a small animal called a scorpion stung him to death. And he was changed into a star picture and placed up in the sky as a warning to all boasters.

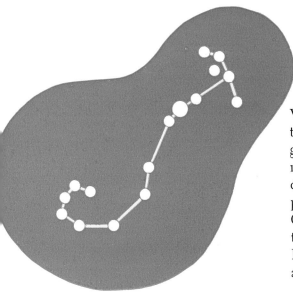

## The Scorpion

When people made up the story about Orion, the mighty hunter, they also imagined that a group of stars which you can see in the summer sky was the scorpion that stung Orion to death. They made up the story that the scorpion still chased Orion through the night skies. Orion goes down in the Western sky just as the Scorpion comes to sight in the Eastern sky. It is easy to imagine that Orion is running away as Scorpion chases him through the sky.

You can see the star group called The Scorpion in the Southern sky during the early midsummer evenings. This picture shows how the stars appear, except, of course, that they actually do not have the lines that connect them in this picture.

This is what the imaginary picture of The Scorpion is supposed to look like.

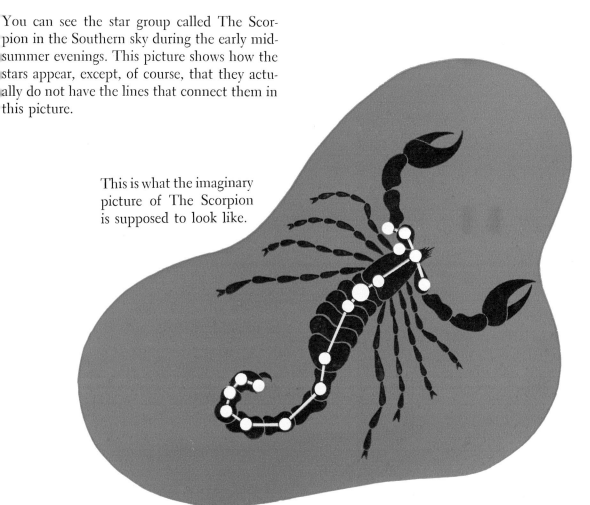

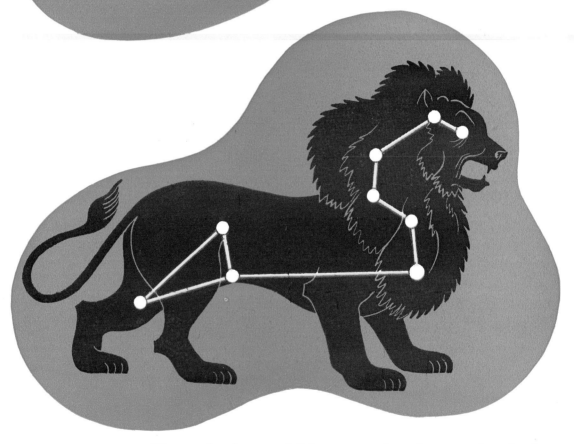

## Leo, the Lion

Herc is a star group which you can see high in the Southern sky in the springtime. If you were looking at this star group today, what would you think it looks like? What would you call it?

The people who named this star group long, long ago, thought that it looked like a fierce lion. So they pretended that it was the famous lion mentioned in the old story about Hercules, an early hero. Hercules was very, very strong. He was given many tasks to do that ordinary people couldn't have done. One of these tasks was to kill a lion whose skin was so tough that no sword, spear, or arrow could possibly go through it. But Hercules, who was as brave as he was strong, fought the lion with his bare hands and finally choked it to death. Ask your parents to find the story of Hercules and have them read to you about the other tasks that Hercules was given to do.

## How Many Stars Can You See in the Sky?

Go outside on some clear, dark night and look up at the sky. Guess how many stars you can see. Dozens? Hundreds? Thousands? Millions? Billions? It may surprise you to know that there are billions of stars in the sky. But you cannot see more than about 2,500 stars with your bare eyes at any one time!

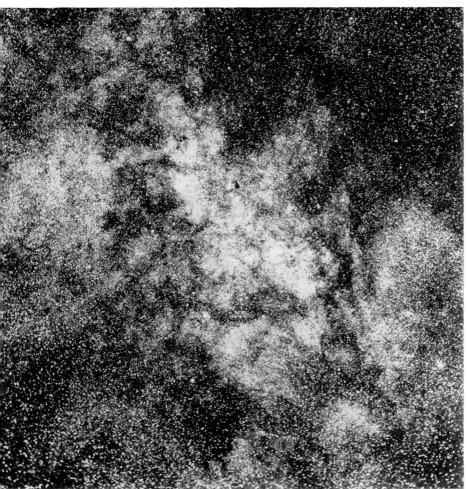

Yerkes Observatory

Of course there are more than 2,500 stars in the sky, but we need a telescope to see them. This picture, taken through a telescope, shows many more stars in just one part of the sky than we can see all over with our bare eyes. It shows a part of the Milky Way. You can see that the Milky Way is really made up of many, many stars.

## How Many Stars Are There?

Yerkes Observatory

If your father has a pair of binoculars, or field glasses, take them with you some night and look at the Milky Way. You will see that it is made up of so many stars that you could never count them all. Most of the stars are very dim, but together they make a path of light across the sky.

Woody Williams

Those who study the sky tell us that there are probably as many stars out in space as there are grains of sand on all the beaches of the earth put together. That is so large a number of stars that no one could even begin to count them.

154

## Traveling by the Stars

The stars have always been used by travelers to help them find their way.

The Bible tells us about a star in the East which guided the wise men to the Christ Child who was born in Bethlehem.

Sailors have always steered their ships at night with the help of the stars.

Desert travelers often travel by night because the desert is cooler at that time. They, too, use the friendly stars to help them find their way.

United Airlines

Today, great airplanes are guided by the stars at night. Airmen use the same stars to guide them that were used by travelers of long ago.

155

## Where Do the Stars Go in the Daytime?

Ask your father to light a match outside on a dark night. You will notice how bright it seems.

Ask him to light another match in the daytime and hold it up toward the sun. It does not seem bright at all. Can you tell why?

You can see the stars at night because the sky is dark. Even the faraway stars shine brightly.

Ewing Galloway

They are still shining in the daytime sky. But we cannot see them because the sun is so bright that it makes the whole sky brighter than the stars. Stars do not go anywhere in the daytime. They stay just where they are, and they shine all the time.

156

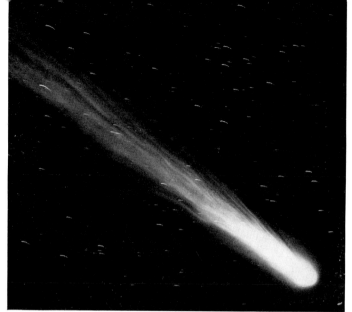

Yerkes Observatory; Mt. Wilson and Palomar Observatories

## Do Some Stars Have Tails?

Once in a while a strange object appears in the sky. It looks like a fuzzy star, but it has a long tail. Night after night it seems to grow bigger. Then, it seems to get smaller and smaller. Finally it disappears altogether. What is this strange thing in the sky? Is it really a star with a tail?

The strange object is not a star at all. It is called a comet, and it goes around the sun much like the earth does. But it isn't solid like the earth. Comets seem to be made of tiny bits of material with long tails made of glowing gases that stream out for millions of miles. There are many comets. But only a few are bright enough to be seen with the bare eyes. This is a picture of a very bright comet.

157

## What Are Shooting Stars?

Shooting stars are not stars at all. They are pieces of rock or metal that go around the sun, much like the earth does. There are so many of them, out in space, that they keep falling into the earth's air. They go so fast that they burn and glow when they hit the air. When you see a falling star, you just see a piece of glowing rock or metal. The real name for a shooting star is meteor, which means "something in the air."

### Have you ever seen meteors?

Billions of meteors come into the earth's air each day, but on most nights we cannot see more than a few in an hour from any one place. But on the nights of August 11, 12, and 13, you may see many of them in an hour if you look toward the Northeast. On those nights many more than usual fall into the earth's air.

## Meteors Which Hit the Earth

Most meteors are so small that they burn to ashes, miles above the earth's surface. But, once in a while, a meteor is too large to burn up entirely. Then it falls to the earth. Meteors that hit the ground are called meteorites. This is a meteorite.

Even the meteors that hit the earth are usually quite small. Only a few are even as big as your fist. But, thousands of years ago, a giant meteor hit the earth and dug a huge hole in the desert of Arizona.

The hole is more than a mile wide and more than 500 feet deep. It is called Meteor Crater.

Chicago Natural History Museum;
Dept. of National Defense, Canada

An even larger meteor crater was found in Canada. It is twice the size of Meteor Crater in Arizona. As you can see, it is filled with water. Can you imagine what *that* meteor must have looked like as it fell, burning, through the sky!

## The Moon Is
## Our Nearest Sky Neighbor

The moon is our nearest neighbor in the sky. That is why it looks so large. If our earth were a hollow globe, it could hold fifty balls the size of our moon. The moon is many millions of times smaller than the sun. But it looks about the same size as the sun in the sky because it is so much nearer to us.

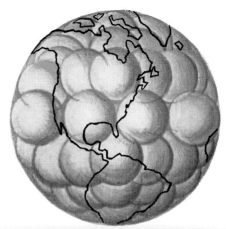

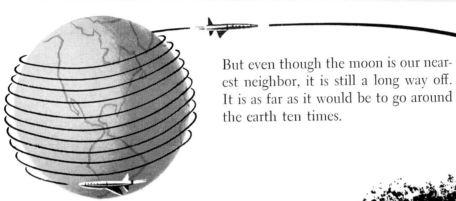

But even though the moon is our nearest neighbor, it is still a long way off. It is as far as it would be to go around the earth ten times.

Let us pretend that we are on a rocket ship traveling at 7 miles a second! It would take you from Christmas day until almost the Fourth of July to get to the sun. But it would take you only nine and a half hours to get to the moon. You could leave at noon on Christmas day and get there in time for a late Christmas supper.

## Many Moons Ago

Years ago, the Indians used the moon to tell time. When they went away they might say "We will return in two moons." Or a story might begin "many moons ago" instead of "once upon a time." To the Indians, a "moon" meant the time it took for the moon to change from a full moon back to a full moon again, or from a new moon to a new moon again.

Today we can tell the time of day by looking at a clock. We can tell what day, week, or month it is by looking at a calendar. Calendars used to be made by watching the moon's changes. The word *month* really comes from the word *moon*. It used to mean the time it took for the full moon to change back to a full moon again. In modern times, a month is just a twelfth of a year. But we keep the old word.

## Is There a Man in the Moon?

There really is no man in the moon, but, we can see light and dark markings on the moon that are made by mountains, craters, and plains. Some people imagine that these markings sometimes look like a man's face. This is supposed to be the man in the moon. But other people imagine they can see a woman's head, or even a rabbit. These are all imaginary pictures, of course, just as you can imagine strange animals in the clouds up in the daytime sky.

Here are the imaginary pictures which people think they can see on the moon. Why don't you look at the moon and see if you can see pictures on it, too?

man pouring
water on fire

rabbit

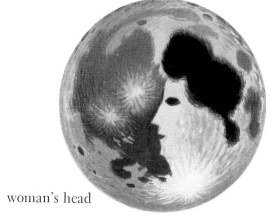

woman's head

162

## What Is the Moon Really Like?

When you look up at the moon, it just looks like a bright ball with some darker spots on it.

But if you look at it through a telescope—it looks like this!

If you use a bigger telescope, it looks like this! Now you can see how rough the surface of the moon really is. It is covered with many deep holes called craters. They look like the meteor craters on our earth. The moon also has many cliffs, as well as many jagged mountains.

Mt. Wilson and Palomar Observatories

This is another picture of the moon, showing the craters even better. There is no air or water on the moon. Nothing grows there. It seems to be a dry, dead world.

# The Changing Moon

If it were not for the sun, we could not see the moon at all. For it has no light of its own. When we look at the moon, we are really seeing sunlight that bounces off it to the earth. It acts like a huge mirror which reflects the light of the sun.

Have you noticed that the moon seems to change its shape? It really doesn't change its shape at all. The moon is round, just like the earth. It also travels around the earth so that it reflects sunlight differently at different times. This makes it seem to change its shape from time to time.

Sometimes you will see the moon in the Western sky, just after sunset. Then it looks like this. It is called a crescent moon.

About a week after you see the crescent moon, you will see the moon overhead just after sunset. Then it looks like this. Now, it is called a half moon.

In another week, the moon is just coming up in the Eastern sky as the sun sets in the west. Then it looks round as a ball.

Here is how the moon seems to change its shape. Once a month, just after sunset, you will see the crescent moon in the Western sky. Then it looks like the picture at the right, below. Every night, at the same time, you will see it farther to the east. And it keeps looking bigger and bigger. In two weeks you will see a completely round moon coming up in the Eastern sky, just after the sun goes down in the west. Now it is called a full moon.

south

The moon keeps coming up later and later after the sun sets and, each night, it looks less and less round. But you would have to stay up later each night to see it at all. Finally, it is a crescent moon again in the evening Western sky, and the process is repeated once more.

# Why Does the Moon Seem to Change Its Shape?

*Try this:* Fasten a white ball on a string and do what the pictures show. It will show you why the moon seems to change its shape.

1. Take the shade off a table lamp. Hold the ball in front of you by its string. Face the lamp as the girl is doing. Now, none of the light can hit the side of the ball you are looking at. So it looks dark.

2. Move the ball slowly to your left. See how the lighted side of the ball begins to show. First you see just a thin sliver of light like the crescent moon. As the ball keeps moving, the lighted part gets bigger and bigger. Your ball will look like a half moon when it has moved as far as the girl has turned.

3. As it keeps moving, more and more of the lighted side of the ball faces you. Finally, you can see all the lighted side. Then it is like a full moon.

4. If you keep moving it, the lighted side becomes less and less. Your ball looks like a half moon again when it has moved as far as the girl has in the picture. Keep it moving and the ball will look like a crescent moon again. Finally it will be all dark on your side, just as it was when you started.

Pluto

Neptune

Uranus

Saturn

Jupiter

**Nine Sky Wanderers**

Mars

Earth

Venus

Mercury

Did you ever see a bright star in the Western sky just after sunset? We sometimes call it the evening star. But it is not a star at all, really.

It is a world, much like our earth. It travels around the sun just as our earth does. There are nine such worlds that we know about. The earth on which we live is one of them.

The nine worlds which travel around the sun are called planets. All nine are shown here. As you can see, they are not all the same size. Which do you think is the largest? Which is the smallest?

## The Planets Are All Different

The planets differ in size and in their distance from the sun. The smallest planet is Mercury. It is also the one that is nearest to the sun.

The planet farthest away from the sun is Pluto. That is why it shows just like a speck in this picture. Even a space ship, traveling seven miles a second, would take almost 17 years to go from the earth to Pluto.

This is Jupiter, the largest of the planets. It is more than a thousand times bigger than the earth.

The most beautiful of the nine planets is Saturn. Whirling around it are beautiful, bright rings made of bits of rock and dust.

Mt. Wilson and Palomar Observatories; Yerkes Observatory

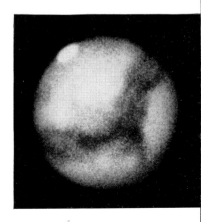

And this is Mars. It is the only planet where living things, like those on the earth, could live. When Mars has its summer, a green color spreads over the planet. This color may come from simple plants called mosses.

168

## What Else Do We Find in the Sky?

This is another gas cloud. This gas cloud does not glow. There are no stars near this gas cloud, so it has no light to reflect. It can be seen, however, because it shows up against the light coming from stars that are behind it.

Far out in space are great clouds of gas. They cannot be seen with your bare eyes. But through giant telescopes we can see them glowing among the distant stars. They glow by reflecting the light from stars that are near them.

Mt. Wilson and Palomar Observatories

Away out in space—far beyond the stars that we can see with our bare eyes—are great groups of stars that seem to float in space like shining islands. This photograph was taken with the largest telescope in the world. It shows one of the star islands away out in space.

## Studying the Sky
## Through the "Big Eye"

The men who study the sky are called astronomers. The places from which they study, or observe, the stars are called observatories. This observatory is in Wisconsin.

Yerkes Observatory

Now you are looking inside an observatory. You are looking at its giant telescope. This is like a big eye which has at one end a special glass called a lens. This gathers a great deal of light so that very faint objects like distant stars are made bright enough to see or to photograph.

At the other end, the telescope has a part you look through which is like a magnifying glass. It makes things seem much bigger than they appear to the bare eye.

Astronomers use many other tools besides telescopes to study the sky. But telescopes are probably the most important of their tools. Without telescopes, it would be impossible to catch enough light to study many of the distant stars. Without telescopes, it would be impossible to see what many objects in the sky are like.

This is an observatory in California where the world's largest telescope is kept. This telescope is sometimes called the Big Eye.

Mt. Wilson and Palomar Observatories

This is what the inside of the California observatory looks like. Do you see how different this giant telescope looks from the one on the page before? That is because this telescope uses a huge, curved mirror, instead of a clear glass lens, to collect light. The mirror is 200 inches across! This is nearly 17 feet. Get a foot ruler and mark out 17 feet on the ground.

This great telescope has made it possible for astronomers to look out into space for far greater distances than before.

## Who Will Be the First Space Man?

The first space man may be you! The first space man will explore the skies, just as Columbus explored the seas when he discovered America in 1492. The Columbus of 1992—the explorer of space—may already be born. But we will need to learn many, many more things before space men are ready for their first trip from our planet.

## Traveling in Space

No one can say for sure, but many people think that we should be able to leave the earth and travel out into space some time in the next fifty years or so. Maybe we can even reach the near-by places in the sky, like the moon, Venus, and Mars. Experiments with rockets like this are helping to make this possible.

There are many ideas about what space ships may look like. These are some of the kinds which have been drawn.

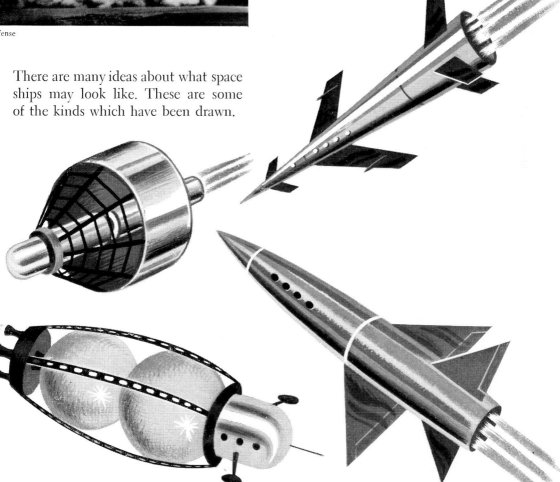

# How Fast Will Space Ships Have to Travel?

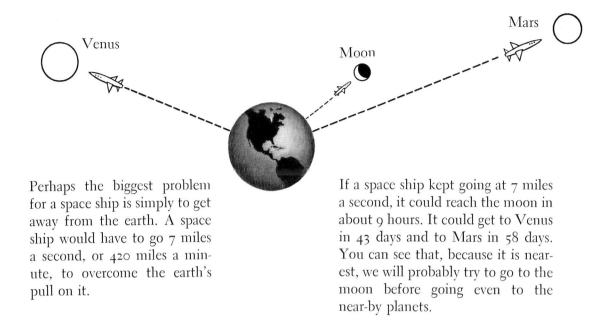

Perhaps the biggest problem for a space ship is simply to get away from the earth. A space ship would have to go 7 miles a second, or 420 miles a minute, to overcome the earth's pull on it.

If a space ship kept going at 7 miles a second, it could reach the moon in about 9 hours. It could get to Venus in 43 days and to Mars in 58 days. You can see that, because it is nearest, we will probably try to go to the moon before going even to the near-by planets.

But, even before we go to the moon, some scientists think that we will build a space station much closer to the earth than the moon. It will go around the earth like another moon. Then, space travelers can take off from the earth and go just to the space station. Then they can take off from there more easily for the moon and planets than if they were to leave directly from the earth, where gravity is so strong.

# THE MACHINES WE USE

Lambert

MACHINES, machines, machines! Big and little machines! Machines for work and play! Machines to dig with, to pound with, to pull with, and to push with! Machines in which we speed over the highways, up into the air, deep into the earth, and even under the water! Machines to help the farmer raise his crops and machines to help your father and mother at home!

Perhaps you have heard someone say that we live in a machine age. That is because we have so many different kinds of machines to help us do things better, faster, and easier than we could without them. Long, long ago, people did almost everything by hand. But, today, you can get a machine to do almost anything you want to do.

What are machines, anyway? How do they work? And what makes them go?

## Machines in the Home

What machines can you find in this picture? Look carefully, and remember that machines help us to do things more easily, more quickly, or better than we could without them.

Can you tell what machines you can see in this picture?

There are machines in this picture, too. Can you name them?

What other machines can you think of that are used in and around the house?

## Digging Machines

The machines on this page are all used for digging. At one time, men had to use simple tools like picks and shovels with which to dig. This work took a long time, and it was hard work. Now, big machines do the work of a hundred men in less time.

A road scraper will smooth rough roads quickly.

This giant bulldozer shovels dirt, pushes things around, and does all sorts of jobs that could hardly be done at all without it.

Have you ever helped dig a garden with a spade? It, too, is a machine.

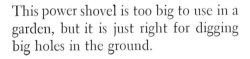

This power shovel is too big to use in a garden, but it is just right for digging big holes in the ground.

Ewing Galloway

Here is a special kind of digging machine. It digs a long, narrow trench in the ground to put pipes in for carrying water, gas, or oil. It can dig as much in an hour as a man with a spade could dig in a week.

178

## Building Machines

Machines make it possible to build things easier and faster, too. Without such machines it would be much more difficult to build offices and factories as fast and strong as we do today.

This truck mixes concrete as it roars down the road from the cement plant to where the concrete is needed. Sand, rocks, water, and cement are mixed in the big tank. The tank goes around and around as it mixes them together.

When the concrete truck gets to where a big building is being made, it pours the concrete into wheelbarrows that are whisked up to the top by this elevator.

Carew, Monkmeyer; Ewing Galloway; U. S. Steel Corp.

Steel and other things that are too big and heavy for the elevator are lifted up by this big crane.

## Some Hand Tools Are Building Machines, Too

There are many kinds of building machines. But among the most important are the simple machines we call tools.

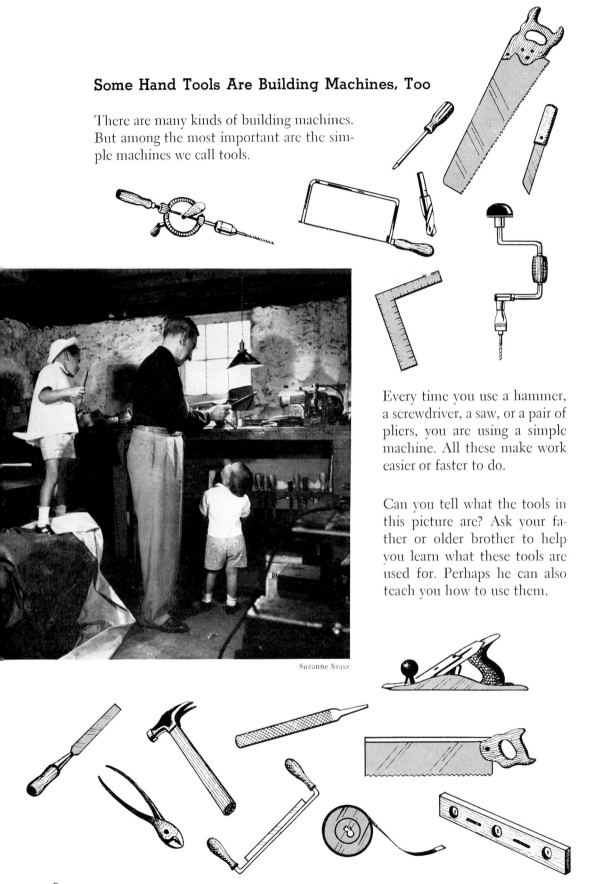

Suzanne Szasz

Every time you use a hammer, a screwdriver, a saw, or a pair of pliers, you are using a simple machine. All these make work easier or faster to do.

Can you tell what the tools in this picture are? Ask your father or older brother to help you learn what these tools are used for. Perhaps he can also teach you how to use them.

180

## Machines on the Farm

There is much work to be done on a farm. Crops have to be planted, taken care of, gathered, and stored. A farmer couldn't get his work done as fast or nearly as well if it were not for the machines that he uses.

The farmer uses a tractor to pull a big plow that breaks up the soil.

Sometimes he uses a disk plow to loosen the soil.

These machines are planting wheat seeds.

This machine is a combine. It is used for reaping wheat. It also separates the grain from the stalks.

J. I. Case Co.; Ewing Galloway

Even the loading of the corn into the farmer's barn can be done by machine.

181

## Machines That Go Places

Airplanes, automobiles, and other machines are made to go places. There are many kinds of such machines. They take us over the water and under it. They take us over the land, and up into the air.

Ships like this one travel over the oceans, rivers, and great lakes of the world. Propellers whirl in the water and push them along.

H. Armstrong Roberts; Fruehauf

A tricycle is a machine, too. You push down with your legs, the wheels go round, and off you go!

When you push the pedals of a bicycle, a chain makes the rear wheel go round and round, and away you go.

A motorcycle is really just a big bicycle with an engine to make it go. The engine does the work, instead of a person's legs.

An automobile or truck isn't much different from a motorcycle. It has four wheels instead of two. But it has an engine that makes the wheels go round, like a motorcycle has.

## A Machine That Flies

The airplane is a machine that really travels fast. Like big ships, it, too, has a propeller. But an airplane's propeller whirls through the air instead of through water.

An airplane's propeller is something like a big fan. It helps to make the airplane move forward. When it is moving fast enough, the wind rushing past the wings causes the airplane to lift up into the air.

If you have a small electric fan and a pair of roller skates, your father can show you how a propeller makes an airplane move forward.

Put a book on two skates, which should be on a smooth floor. Have your father put the fan on the book, like this. Be sure the fan is turned off.

Now have him connect the fan so that it starts working. **Don't get near it or you might be cut by the fan blades.** See how the propeller moves your machine across the floor. Before the fan and skates hit something, your father will pull out the electric cord.

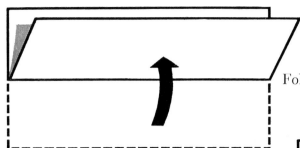

Fold a piece of writing paper like this.

Now, open it up and fold it like this so that it makes a point.

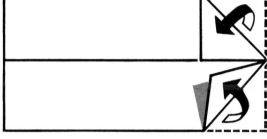

Fold each side down, again, so that the point gets longer, like this.

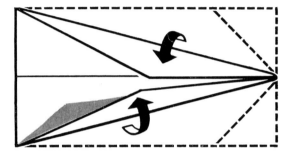

Fold again on the center crease. Now it looks like this.

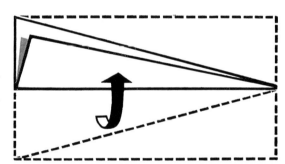

Then fold each side of the paper down, like this, to make the wings.

Your paper airplane, when finished, should look like this. It doesn't have a propeller, so you must hold it as the boy is doing, and throw it forward to make it fly. If it dives down, bend the tips of the wings up a little.

## A Machine
## That Goes Under the Water

A submarine is a machine that is made to go places under the water. Do you know what makes it go down under the water and what makes it come up again?

A submarine has several big tanks full of air that keep it floating.

When the submarine's crew wants to go under the water, the men close a cover down tight. Then they open up the air tank and let the water pour in. The air is pushed out as the water pours in. This makes the submarine heavy, and it sinks.

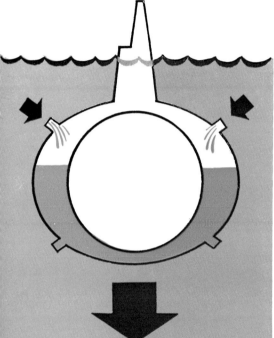

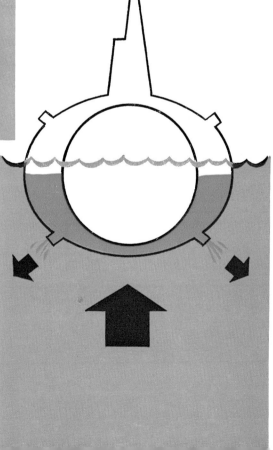

When they want to come up again, the men pass air from storage tanks into the big tank. The air pushes the water out and makes the submarine lighter, so that it rises to the surface.

185

## Machines to Play With

Many things we play with are really machines. Here are some of them.

The teeter-totter is a machine on which almost everyone has played.

Wind-up toys work when you wind up a big spring.

And a play sweeper works just like mother's.

A bow shoots arrows much faster and straighter than you can throw them.

A toy derrick works almost like a real one.

H. Armstrong Roberts; Ewing Galloway

Even a bat is a machine. It hits the ball much harder than you could without it.

186

## Which Is Easier?

Most of the machines we use help us do our work easier and faster. Without machines, some things couldn't be done!

Did you ever try pulling a nail from a board with your bare hands? If the nail is in deep, it just won't come out.

But if you use a claw hammer, as this boy is doing, it is easy.

Did your mother ever send you to the grocery store for groceries? Carrying home a big sack full of groceries in your arms is hard work.

Pulling the same sack of groceries home in a wagon, whose wheels go round and round, makes the work easy.

Edith Loder

Try cracking a nut between your fingers. Now, try cracking the nut with a nutcracker. Which is easier?

187

Hibbs

## Which Is Faster?

Sometimes we use machines, especially to do things faster. The work we do without machines is usually not nearly as fast as when we do it with machines.

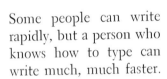

Maybe you can run very fast, but you can go even faster on a bicycle.

Some people can write rapidly, but a person who knows how to type can write much, much faster.

This man is rowing a boat. But if you really want to go fast, you can get into a motorboat such as this one. It has an engine that turns a propeller. This machine makes the boat zoom through the water!

188

# The Wheel,
# One of Man's Greatest Inventions

Stop and think, for a moment, of the many ways in which wheels are used. What would the world be like if there were no wheels? There could be no tricycles, cars, trains, airplanes, or wagons. But that is not all. Almost all important machines, from typewriters to steam shovels and elevators, have several wheels in them to make them work.

The wheel is one of our simplest machines. But it is also one of man's greatest inventions. Try this and you will see why—

Put all your toys in a big box. Try to push it across the floor.

Now, put all your toys in a wagon and push it across the floor. Is it easier or harder than with the box? Do you see why? A wagon is a wheel machine. When a thing rolls on wheels, it goes much more easily than when it has to be dragged along.

Aigner

189

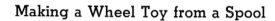

## Making a Wheel Toy from a Spool

Spool automobiles are easy to make and lots of fun to play with. They go by themselves and will even climb a hill.

You will need an empty spool; two wooden kitchen matchsticks; a small piece of soap; and a rubber band for the motor.

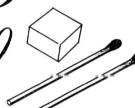

Have a little notch cut across one end of the spool, like this.

Put the rubber band through the hole in the spool. Break one of your matchsticks and stick a piece through the loop of the rubber band at the notched end of the spool.

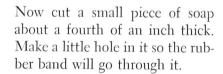

Now cut a small piece of soap about a fourth of an inch thick. Make a little hole in it so the rubber band will go through it.

Put the rubber band through the piece of soap at the unnotched end of the spool and then put a long matchstick through the loop. Now your spool automobile is done. It should look like this.

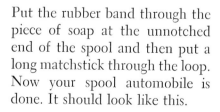

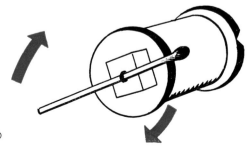

Wind up the rubber-band motor by turning the long matchstick around and around. Put the spool on a table top and watch it go!

## Wheels Need Axles Before They Will Work

Would these wheels do any good? Why?

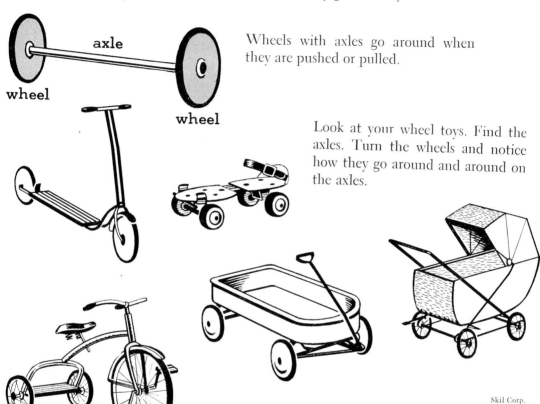

axle

wheel

wheel

Wheels with axles go around when they are pushed or pulled.

Look at your wheel toys. Find the axles. Turn the wheels and notice how they go around and around on the axles.

Sometimes wheels are fastened tightly to their axles. The stiff sandpaper wheel in this picture is fastened to its axle, which goes around very fast when the motor is turned on.

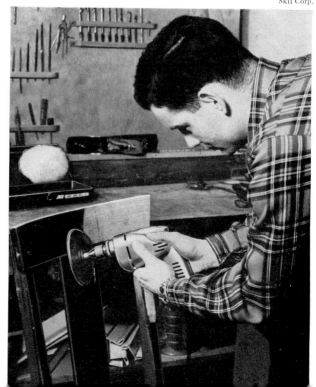

## Wheels That Turn, But Go Nowhere

Some wheels do not go anywhere; yet they work for us.

The steering wheel in your car doesn't roll anywhere, but you couldn't steer the car without it.

This water wheel doesn't go anywhere except around and around, but it grinds flour for the miller.

This wheel is a grindstone. It is used to sharpen tools.

Some water-faucet handles are made like this. Turning the wheel-handle turns the water on and off.

Miller, FPG; Bauer, Cushing; Aigner; Hibbs

A spool is a wheel. Did you ever watch the spool of thread when your mother was using the sewing machine? It goes around and around as the thread is used up.

## Wheels with Teeth

Wheels with teeth are found on many machines. Can you tell how they work? Do you see how one wheel with teeth makes another one go around?

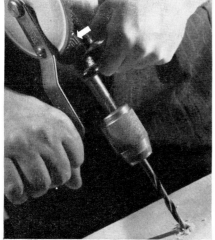

An egg beater shows you how wheels with teeth work. What other machines with toothed wheels does your mother use?

Your father probably uses machines with toothed wheels, too. This hand drill is used to bore holes. It has wheels with teeth on the sides of the rim.

Ewing Galloway; Hobart, Monkmeyer; H. Armstrong Robert; Suzanne Szasz; Aigner

Sometimes toothed wheels are made so that a chain connects them. Then, when you turn one wheel around, the chain turns the other wheel. That is how a bicycle works.

If you want to see many wheels with teeth, all working together, have your father take the cover off an old alarm clock so that you can see how the insides look.

## Pulling with Pulleys

Pulleys are just wheels on axles, but they have grooves in the rims, or edges, so that ropes can go around them without slipping off. Pulleys have many important uses.

This woman can hang out her washing to dry without going out of doors. Pulleys carry the wash out on the line when she pulls on the rope.

If it weren't for the pulley fastened to the top of the barn, this farmer would have to carry his hay up to the haymow a bundle at a time.

Pulleys can be fixed up so that big loads can be pulled or lifted easily. These men tried to lift a heavy load with a single pulley. But the load was too heavy for them. So they fixed up several pulleys together. Now the rope goes around the bottom pulleys four times. This takes much less strength for the men to lift the heavy load.

Ewing Galloway

194

# Fun with Pulleys

Pulleys are fun to play with. You will need a clothesline. You also will need

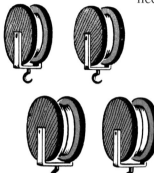

two single pulleys that look like this

two double pulleys that look like this

Fasten one of the single pulleys up like this. Try lifting up a book or toy car with it.

Now fasten two of the single pulleys like this. Do you notice that the load is easier to lift than with one pulley? It is about twice as easy to lift.

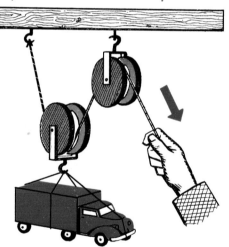

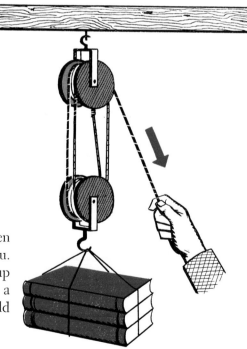

If you want to lift a big load very easily, fasten your pulleys like this. Get your father to help you. Now try lifting up a heavy toy or brick. It goes up easily. You could lift almost four times as heavy a load with your pulleys fixed this way as you could without them.

## How to Lift a Big Weight with One Finger

Here is how to have fun with your friends! Tie four or five heavy books together with a string. Ask one of your friends if he thinks you can lift the books with one finger. He is almost sure to say "No, of course not! Those books are much too heavy for anyone to lift with one finger!"

Actually, the books **are** too heavy to lift with one finger, if you try to lift like this.

But here is how you can really do it. Get a broom or mop. Fasten the pile of books to one end of the broom or mop handle. Use a strong string that is long enough to let you put the handle over the back of a chair, like this.

Aigner

Be sure that most of the broom handle is on **your** side of the chair as in the picture. Now, press down with your finger on the **end** of the broom handle. The books are lifted almost as easily as if they were feathers.

When you use a stick or bar in this way, you are using another kind of simple machine. It is called a lever. Levers are among the most important machines we have.

## How a Lever Works Best

Try to lift the books with the chair back moved near to you, like this.

Now try it with the chair back moved near to the books, like this.

Try it with the chair back moved so that it is the same distance between the books and your hand, like this.

Which way was the easiest way to lift the books?

If you want to lift a big weight with a lever, always put whatever your lever rests on near to the weight and far from your hands.

## How We Use Levers

Sometimes we use levers to play with. A teeter-totter is a lever. If you teeter-totter with someone bigger than you, have him get nearer to the center. Then you will balance each other.

A wrench is a lever, too.

So is a pump handle.

Sometimes we get jars of food with covers on them that have to be taken off by prying them up. Then we use the back of a table knife for a lever.

Edith Loder; Aigner; Ewing Galloway; Hibbs

Sometimes two levers are fastened together to make a tool. A pair of scissors is just two levers fastened together. When you squeeze the handles of the scissors together, the blades slide past each other and cut things easily.

## More Levers

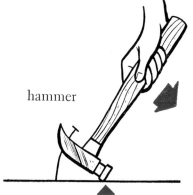

hammer

Hibbs

toy steam shovel

crowbar in use

shovel

rake

bicycle pedal

handle bars
of tricycle

pliers

canoes being paddled

199

## Hill Machines

Which is easier?

To pull a wagon up a steep, rough slope like this

. . . or to pull it up a slanting board like this? Try it and find out!

When you use a slanting board to make a hill in order to raise something from a lower place to a higher place, the board becomes a machine—a hill machine!

## How We Use Hill Machines

It is much easier to roll or slide weights up a slanting board than to lift them straight up. Hill machines, like this one, are used all the time to move weights up higher.

When roads are made over mountainsides, they zigzag back and forth. Then cars can go up a slanting road. If the road went straight up the mountainside, cars would slip and slide. They wouldn't have enough power to climb.

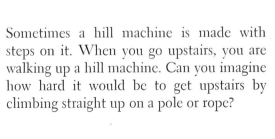

Sometimes a hill machine is used to get from a high place to a lower place safely and swiftly.

Standard Oil Co. of N. J.; Hibbs; Suzanne Szasz

Sometimes a hill machine is made with steps on it. When you go upstairs, you are walking up a hill machine. Can you imagine how hard it would be to get upstairs by climbing straight up on a pole or rope?

201

## Fun with a Homemade Hill Machine

Boys and girls who have had fun on a roller coaster have really been on a hill machine. You can have fun, too, in making your own toy roller coaster. All you need is a garden hose for the tracks and a small ball for the car that goes up and down along the tracks.

Youngman, Black Sta

First, double your garden hose, like this.

Then put the doubled hose over a garden chair, boxes, or bricks, so that it goes up and down, like this. Be sure that the hoses are tight together, so your little ball will not fall through between them.

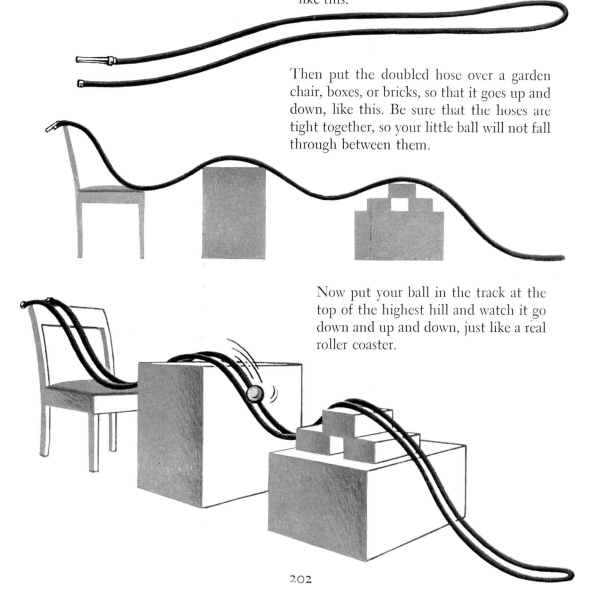

Now put your ball in the track at the top of the highest hill and watch it go down and up and down, just like a real roller coaster.

## Screws Are Machines, Too

If you will look carefully at a screw, you will see that the edges go around and around. Run your fingernail along the edge, starting at the point. You will find that the edge slowly climbs to the top of the screw. A screw is a kind of hill machine. The slanting hill is wrapped around and around the screw.

A bolt is a screw machine, too. It screws into a little piece of metal called a nut. When you tighten the nut, the bolt will hold things tightly together.

If your mother has a food grinder that looks like this, turn the handle. As you do so, notice how the screw on the inside, pushes the food along.

FPG.; Hibbs; Aigner

When you turn the handle on this vise, it turns a screw that forces the jaws together so that they will hold things tightly.

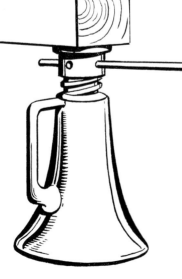

This builder's jack makes it easy to lift heavy weights off the ground. Do you see why?

203

## Machines with Sharp Edges and Points

These men are splitting a log. They are pounding in a piece of metal that is shaped something like a piece of pie. A pie-shaped piece of metal is called a wedge. This wedge keeps forcing the wood apart until the log splits in two.

An axe is another wedge machine with a sharp edge. It is used for cutting wood.

This boy is whittling a stick with a pocket-knife. The knife has a sharp edge. Its shape is that of a wedge.

Aigner; H. Armstrong Roberts

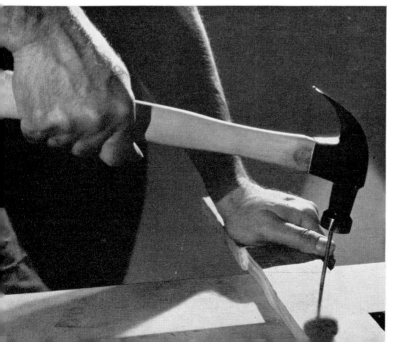

Even a nail is a wedge machine. The sharp point pushes its way into the wood when the nail is hammered.

Needles and pins are wedge machines, too. Imagine trying to sew with a needle that didn't have a sharp point!

204

## Several Machines in One

One of the most interesting things about many machines is that they are often made up of a number of simple machines such as wheels, levers, and wedges.

Take a lawnmower, for example

. . . the handle is just a lever

. . . it has two big wheels to run on

. . . many little wheels with teeth

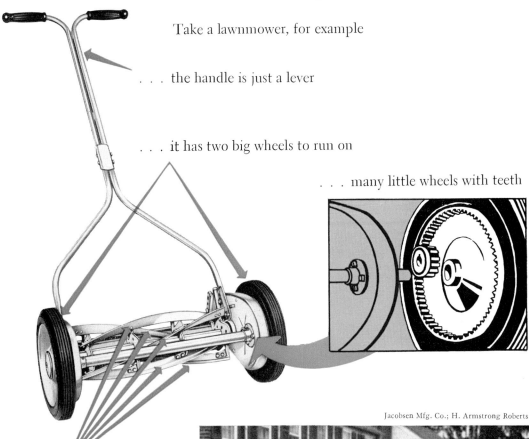

Jacobsen Mfg. Co.; H. Armstrong Roberts

. . . it has several cutting blades which are wedges

. . . and the whole thing is put together with screws and bolts.

Some lawnmowers are run with engines. But even the engine is made of wheels, toothed wheels, levers, and screw machines.

205

## Machines Will Not Work by Themselves

This garden spade is not doing any work.

These automobiles are not moving.

Neither are these freight cars.

This tractor is doing no work.

Ewing Galloway

Why aren't these machines doing any work? Are they lazy? Of course not! Machines cannot do work by themselves. Somebody will have to work to make the spade work. The engines of cars and the tractor have to be turned on before they will do work. The freight cars cannot move until the railroad engine hooks on to them and pulls them. Machines will not work by themselves.

## Animal Muscles Make Some Machines Work

In all parts of the world, animals are used in various ways by man to help him in his work.

In pioneer days, there were no automobiles or trucks. Horses were used in pulling stagecoaches and covered wagons. Horses are still used in many ways.

Ewing Galloway; H. Armstrong Roberts

In Alaska, dogs are used by the Eskimos to pull their sleds.

The water buffalo is used in the Philippine Islands and other countries. This cart is loaded with fiber for making rope.

## We Use Our Own Muscles to Make Other Machines Work

These people are all using their own muscles to make machines work. Can you think of other machines that people work with their own muscles?

Cushing; Hibbs; Ewing Galloway

## Air Works for Us in Some Machines

Sometimes air is used to work our machines. The wind turns this windmill which is fastened by levers to a pump that pumps water up from a well.

Ewing Galloway

Sometimes we suck the air out of things to make them work. Do you know what happens when you suck milk or an ice-cream soda through a straw?

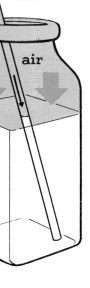

When you put the straw in the milk bottle, there is air in the upper part of it. Air also pushes down on the milk in the bottle.

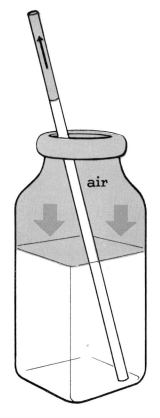

When you suck on the straw, you pull out some of the air that is in it. When this happens, the air pushing down on the milk pushes the milk up the straw and into your mouth.

Your mother's vacuum cleaner has a fan that blows air into the bag. This sucks the air out from the opening on the floor. Dirt is then sucked up with the air.

bag        fan

air

209

## We Use Air Under Pressure in Other Machines

Blow up a balloon and let it go. It will swoosh around the room like a jet airplane. When you blew up the balloon, you forced the air together, or compressed it. When you let the balloon go, the compressed air swooshed the balloon around the room.

A jet airplane works the same way. Only, instead of compressed air, it uses hot, burning gases.

Did you ever see a workman breaking up a street with a big drill like this? It is called a pneumatic drill. Air under pressure goes through the hose into the big drill and makes it go brr! brr! brr! brr! as it pounds into the concrete.

U. S. Air Force; Ewing Galloway

### How to make a compressed-air elevator:

Place a book on an empty water bottle as shown here. Blow into the tube. You will find that the book will go up! It is the pressure of the air in the water bottle which lifts the book.

## Machines Run by Liquids

When the barber raises the barber chair before giving you a haircut, he works a lever that pumps oil into a tank under the chair. It is this oil that makes the chair rise.

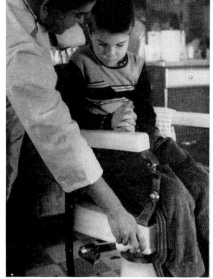

When the filling-station man lifts your car up to grease it, oil goes into a big tank under the car lift. Up the car goes, just like your water-bottle elevator and the barber chair.

Running water makes this lawn sprinkler work. The water rushes out of the openings in one direction, and makes the top of the sprinkler whirl around in the other direction.

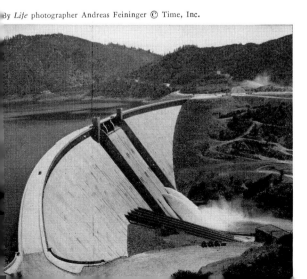

Sometimes rivers are dammed up to make electricity. The water behind the dam rushes down huge pipes. At the bottom of the pipes are water wheels. The falling water makes them whirl very fast. The water wheels are fastened to huge machines that make electricity.

## How to Make a Water Wheel

Have mother give you a lid cut from a large tin can. Be careful that you do not cut yourself on the sharp edge. Punch a hole in the center of the lid with a nail.

Ask your father to cut slits in the lid with a pair of tin snips or old scissors. Then your lid will look like this.

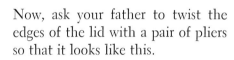

Now, ask your father to twist the edges of the lid with a pair of pliers so that it looks like this.

Put a small nail through the hole at the center of the lid. Pound the nail a little way into a board, like this. Now your water wheel is ready to work.

Hold the water wheel in front of the garden hose or under a faucet. Watch it whirl!

## Heat Runs Many of Our Machines

Sometimes the water in a teakettle boils so hard that the steam makes the cover bounce up and down. By heating water, we can make steam and use it to run machines.

Steam makes this locomotive go. Coal or oil is burned to change water into steam. The steam pushes against a sort of big iron can, called a piston. This makes the piston go back and forth very fast. A lever fastened to the piston makes the wheels go round and round.

This big digging machine runs from heat made by burning oil.

Ewing Galloway; Titcomb, Black Star; Northwest Airlines

Airplanes burn gasoline instead of coal or oil. The gasoline burns and makes hot gases which push the pistons. Levers connect the pistons to the propeller.

213

## Electricity Works for Us, Too

All the things on this page work by electricity. In different parts of your house, usually in the walls, there are electric outlets. When your mother or father plugs in a lamp or something else, its wires connect with wires that go through the walls of your house to the electric outlet. All you have to do then is to turn on the switch and the electricity goes to work.

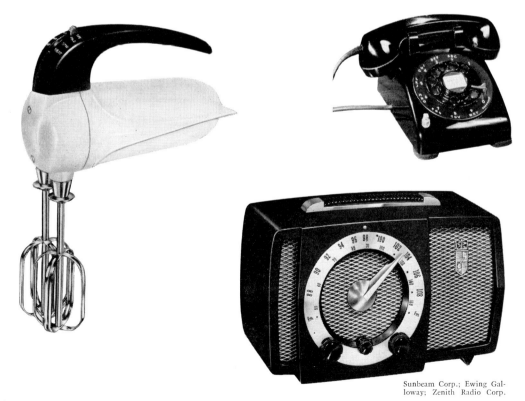

Sunbeam Corp.; Ewing Galloway; Zenith Radio Corp.

## Where Does Electricity Come From?

Lightning is a kind of electricity. It is very powerful, but it comes and goes so fast that there is no way we can put it to use.

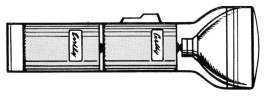

One way we get electricity is from things called dry cells. If you will look inside a flashlight you will see the dry cells. They have chemicals in them that produce electricity which you use when you press the button.

Your automobile has a different kind of electric cell. It is called a storage battery. It makes electricity from chemicals, too.

Hobart, Monkmeyer; Aigner; Ewing Galloway

Most of the electricity we use is made by big machines called generators. Some are very large and produce enough electricity for whole towns and cities. The electricity you use in your home was probably produced by a big generator.

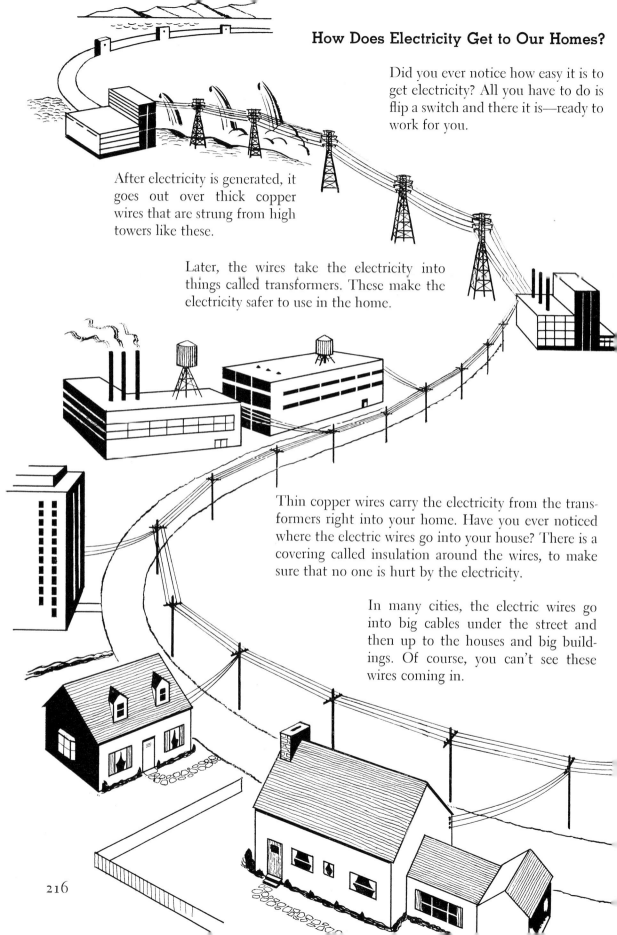

# How Does Electricity Get to Our Homes?

Did you ever notice how easy it is to get electricity? All you have to do is flip a switch and there it is—ready to work for you.

After electricity is generated, it goes out over thick copper wires that are strung from high towers like these.

Later, the wires take the electricity into things called transformers. These make the electricity safer to use in the home.

Thin copper wires carry the electricity from the transformers right into your home. Have you ever noticed where the electric wires go into your house? There is a covering called insulation around the wires, to make sure that no one is hurt by the electricity.

In many cities, the electric wires go into big cables under the street and then up to the houses and big buildings. Of course, you can't see these wires coming in.

## How to Make Electricity
## Move Things

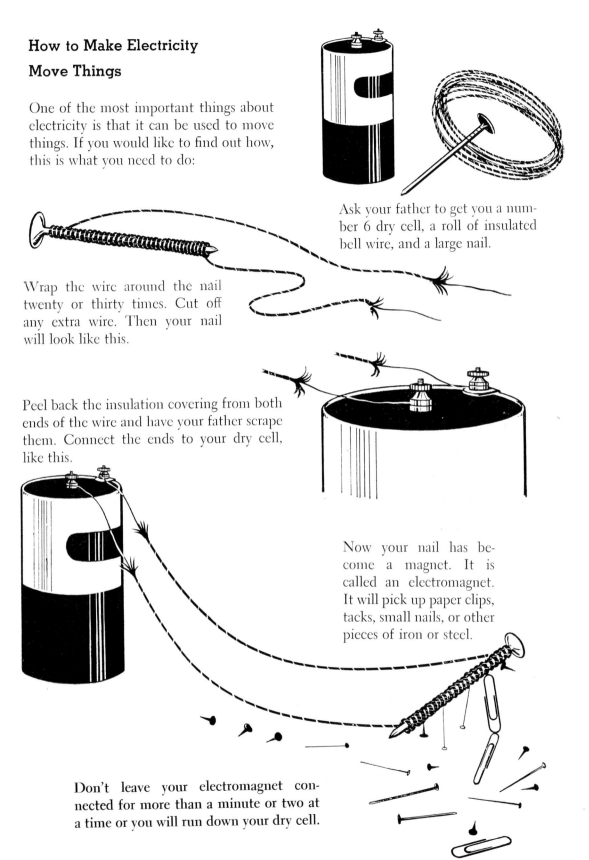

One of the most important things about electricity is that it can be used to move things. If you would like to find out how, this is what you need to do:

Ask your father to get you a number 6 dry cell, a roll of insulated bell wire, and a large nail.

Wrap the wire around the nail twenty or thirty times. Cut off any extra wire. Then your nail will look like this.

Peel back the insulation covering from both ends of the wire and have your father scrape them. Connect the ends to your dry cell, like this.

Now your nail has become a magnet. It is called an electromagnet. It will pick up paper clips, tacks, small nails, or other pieces of iron or steel.

Don't leave your electromagnet connected for more than a minute or two at a time or you will run down your dry cell.

## Putting Magnets to Work

Electromagnets are used for all sorts of things.

They make doorbells ring.

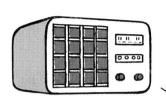

Your radio has several electromagnets in it.

So does a television set.

Your telephone wouldn't work without electromagnets.

Moore, Black Star

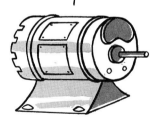

Electromagnets make an electric motor work. And think of all the machines that use electric motors.

This crane is lifting scrap metal with a huge electromagnet.

## How Electricity Heats Things

One of the ways we put electricity to work is to heat things for us.

When electricity flows through some kinds of wires, they get red hot. Have you ever seen the wires in a toaster get hot?

Some people cook with electricity.

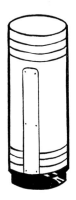

This water heater works with electricity.

This electric heater would warm you up fast.

And some people even have electric blankets to keep them warm in bed.

Aigner; H. Armstrong Roberts

Ask your mother to help you find all the ways you use electricity to make heat in your home.

## Electricity Can Be Changed into Light

When electricity goes through the very thin wire inside this light bulb, the wire gets **white** hot and gives off light.

In the old days, electric-light bulbs were made of clear glass and you could easily see the thin wires glowing white hot.

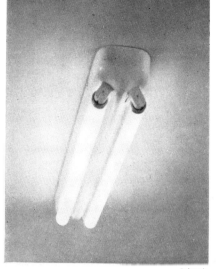

Sylvania

Sometimes, today, we use fluorescent tubes instead of light bulbs. The electricity makes chemicals glow to give light in fluorescent tubes.

### Changing Electricity to Light with a Dry Cell

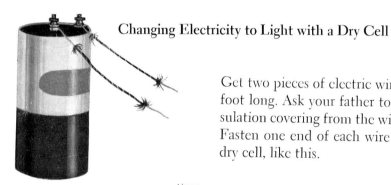

Get two pieces of electric wire, each about a foot long. Ask your father to remove the insulation covering from the wires at each end. Fasten one end of each wire to a number 6 dry cell, like this.

Aigner

Get a light bulb from a flashlight. Hold the bare end of one wire tightly against the metal side of the light bulb. Hold the bare end of the other wire tightly against the little tip at the bottom of the bulb. What happens?

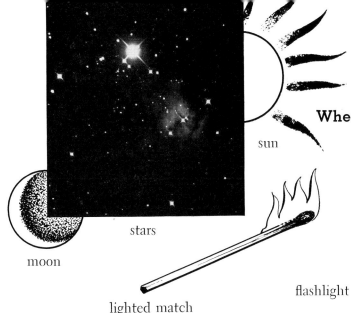

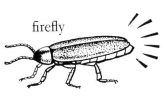
firefly

sun

moon

stars

## Where Else Does Light Come From?

All these things give us light. Can you tell which ones give off heat, too.

lighted match

flashlight

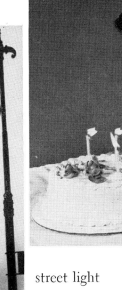
candles

street light

bonfire

kerosene lamp

## Putting Light to Work

We use light to chase away the darkness

Black Star; Pinney, Monkmeyer; Cushing

. . . and to take pictures.

And we study the sun, moon, stars, and the planets by the light they give.

Great floodlights make it possible to play baseball, football, and other games at night.

Tell about other ways in which we use light.

## What Is Sound?

Do you know what sound is?
Try this to find out:

Stretch a rubber band around a small box without a cover and pluck it. Do you hear a sound? Can you see the rubber band move back and forth? This is what makes the sound as it pushes the air around it. We call this back and forth movement vibration.

Tap the edge of a pan lid with a stick. Do you feel it vibrate?

Hibbs; Aigner

Feel your father's voice box at the front of his neck when he is talking or singing. Have him growl real low and then squeak real high. Do you feel the difference in the way his voice box vibrates?

Sounds are made by things that vibrate. Sound is just vibrations that go into your ears. You will find an interesting section, FUN WITH SOUND AND RHYTHM, in CHILDCRAFT, Volume 11, pages 3 to 26.

## How Sound Works for Us

We use sound in many ways. Of course, we make sound into words so that we can understand each other. Here are some other ways we put sound to work for us:

Fire trucks, ambulances, and police cars have sirens which make such a loud sound we all can hear it and get out of the way.

If you want to talk with someone in another town, you use a telephone. The telephone changes your voice vibrations to electric vibrations which go down the wire. At the other end, the electric vibrations are changed back to sound vibrations.

It is sound, too, which makes it possible for you to hear programs over your radio.

Ewing Galloway; General Electric

224

# HOW SCIENCE
# AND INDUSTRY
# HELP US

Northern Pacific Railway

As you walk along the streets in your town, you pass all kinds of stores. In the windows you may see toys, candy, food, clothes, furniture, radios, television sets, machines, cars, and many, many other things.

When your father and mother passed the stores when they were children, perhaps the things they saw in the windows were different. Do you think they saw toy space helmets, toy jet planes, television sets, and plastic dishes? Ask them.

Men and women have always liked to discover and to make things. Those who discover new things and new ways of doing things are called scientists and inventors. What they learn and discover has to be tried out carefully, again and again, to make sure that it will work.

Then other men in business and industry find ways to use these discoveries for making things we want and need. The things we buy in stores have been made possible because science and industry are partners working together.

## Where Do They Come From?

Look at the pictures of all the things shown on this page. Where did they come from? From what are they made? How are they made?

You may say that people made them. But what materials did they use and where did they come from? Some materials came from the earth, some from water, and some from things which grow on the earth.

Can you tell what the things shown here are made of?

## The Foods We Eat

Suppose that you had lived long ago in early pioneer days! Things would have been very different, wouldn't they? Perhaps there would be no store of any kind for miles and miles and miles.

Then how would you get your food? You would have to hunt and fish. You would gather wild fruit in the summer and nuts in the fall. Perhaps you would even raise vegetables and keep animals.

Now suppose a boy who lived in pioneer days were to live with you today. How surprised he would be to learn that people are paid for the work they do! He would be even more surprised that they can use the money to buy all kinds of food at the store.

228

# Where Does Our Food Come From?

The vegetables you eat are grown in gardens and fields.

Apples, pears, peaches, oranges, plums, and other fruit grow on trees and bushes.

Hens give us eggs and cows give us milk. The milk is taken to the dairy. There it is made safe to drink, and it is put into bottles and cartons. Some of it is made into cream, butter, and cheese.

Animals of all kinds give us meat.

Cereals and breads are made from wheat, oats, and corn that grow in the fields.

## Some of Our Food Comes from the Water

Much of the food we eat comes from fresh water which you find in rivers and lakes. Much more comes from the salt water of the ocean.

Here are some of the fish we can catch in the rivers and lakes.

smelt

catfish

salmon

whitefish

trout

These fishes are caught in the salt water of the ocean. Can you think of any others?

pompano

cod

mackerel

sole

haddock

We get shellfish, too, from the ocean.

lobster

crab

clam

oyster

shrimp

And here are some of the things with which we can catch water creatures.

net

fishing rod

oyster tongs

hooks

rice

bananas

Ewing Galloway

coffee

## Foods from Faraway Places

Some of the foods we eat come from faraway places. Some come from lands across the sea. Others come from places in our own country which may be a long way from where we live. See if your father or mother can help you find out where all these foods come from.

oranges

lemons

brazil nuts

sugar

tea

pineapples

231

## What Happens to the Food That Is Grown on the Farm?

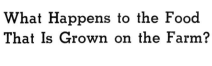

Two big crops that are grown on the farm are corn and wheat. When they are ripe, they are cut. Much of the wheat goes to the flour mills, where it is made into flour. This flour is used by your mother and by the bakery to make bread, cake, rolls, pancakes, and other things to eat.

Some of the corn and wheat goes to the places where breakfast foods are prepared.

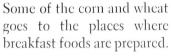

General Mills; H. Armstrong Roberts

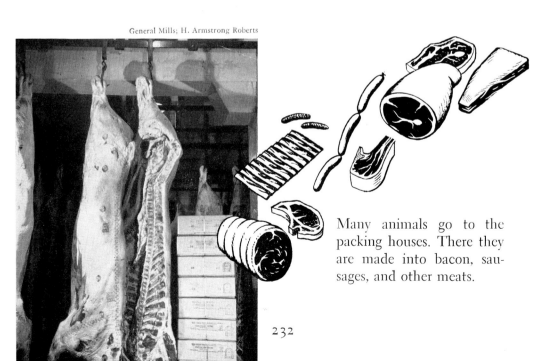

Many animals go to the packing houses. There they are made into bacon, sausages, and other meats.

## How Are Foods Kept from Spoiling?

Did you ever wonder how the Indians and the pioneers kept food from spoiling? They had no refrigerators then and no canned foods. So they learned how to salt, dry, and smoke some of the food they ate.

What the Indians and pioneers once did, we still do. We can buy fish, sausages, bacon, ham, and even turkey which have been salted or smoked. Fruits like grapes and plums are dried to give us raisins and prunes.

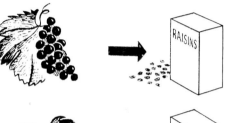

American Can Co.; International Harvester Co.

Your mother may keep fruit and vegetables from spoiling, too, by canning them in jars. They also are put in tin cans in big canning factories. Even fish and meats are canned. What kinds of foods can you name that you can buy in cans?

At the store or at home, you may find food placed in a freezer like this to keep it from spoiling.

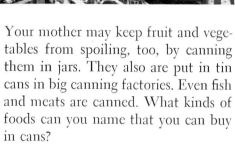

233

## Keeping Fresh Foods Fresh

But we need to keep fresh foods fresh, too, until they are brought to the store. And we need to keep them fresh at home until they are cooked.

One of the best ways to keep fresh foods fresh is to keep them cold. So we have refrigerator cars on the railroad, refrigerator rooms on ships, and refrigerator trucks on the roads. Fruits, vegetables, and meats that are sent in such cars, ships, and trucks are kept cool and fresh for us to use.

Meat is kept cold at the store, and in butcher shops, in cold places like this.

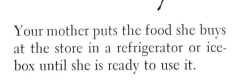

Great Northern Railroad; Fruehauf; Jewel Food Stores; Ewing Galloway

Your mother puts the food she buys at the store in a refrigerator or icebox until she is ready to use it.

234

green and
yellow vegetables

oranges, tomatoes,
grapefruits, lemons

potatoes, other fruits,
and vegetables

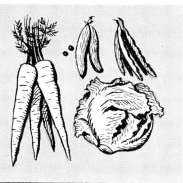

## The Foods You Should Eat

To grow strong and healthy, we need some of each of these seven kinds of food every day. Working together, people in science and in business make it possible for us to buy these foods in easy-to-use form at the store.

milk
and
milk
products

meat
fish
eggs
poultry

bread
flour
cereals

butter and
margarine

J. C. Allen and Son;
Jewel Food Stores

235

Lapham, Publix

## The Clothes We Wear

Look at these pictures. Can you tell of what materials the clothes are made? Some are made from plants which grow in the fields. Some are made from wool, and some are made from the skins of animals. What materials do you think each is made of?

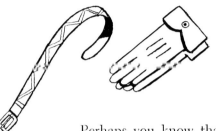

Perhaps you know that scientists and others learned how to use different materials for making clothes. They also learned how to make them in many colors. Machines were invented for making cloth faster than it could be made by hand. Then factories were built where workers could use the machines.

Ewing Galloway

236

## Woolen Clothes to Keep You Warm

Some of the clothes you wear are made from wool. We wear woolen clothes in the winter, and when it is cold, because they help to keep us warm.

The wool that grows on sheep is clipped once each year. This does not hurt the sheep, for it is like having a haircut.

After this wool has been washed, the fibers are loosened and combed out into threads. These are twisted together to make woolen yarn.

H. Armstrong Roberts; Wool Bureau, Inc.; Ewing Galloway

This yarn is woven into cloth from which woolen clothes are made.

Ask your mother to give you some woolen yarn. Untwist it so you can see how it was put together. Pull out some tufts. Now try to twist them together to make yarn like that which your mother gave you.

237

## Cotton Clothes to Keep You Cool

Some of the clothes you wear are made of cotton. We wear cotton clothes in summer, or when it is hot, because they help to keep us cool.

Did you know that cotton grows on plants? The fluffy cotton is picked either by hand or by machine.

After the seeds have been taken out of the cotton, it is packed in bundles called bales.

International Harvester Co.; Soil Conservation Service; Pepperell Mfg. Co.

In the cotton mill, the cotton fibers are twisted into thread on spindles such as these. The cotton thread is then woven into cloth.

238

Woolen and cotton yarn are made into cloth by big machines called looms. These looms weave the woolen or cotton cloth by crisscrossing the threads like this.

You can weave a potholder in this same way. All you have to do is to go to the store and buy a small loom like this. When you buy the loom, you will find a piece of paper inside the box. This will tell you exactly what to weave and how to weave it.

## Silk for Dressing Up

Silk is a soft and beautiful cloth. It is used for making dresses, stockings, ties, shirts, and other clothes. It costs more than cotton and wool, so we do not use silk clothes for everyday work. Here are a few things made from silk. Can you think of others?

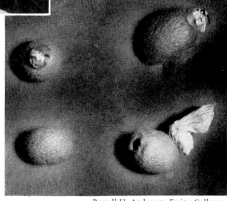

Perhaps you will be surprised to learn that silk is made by caterpillars, called silkworms. They grow by eating the leaves that grow on the mulberry tree.

When the silkworm is ready to become a moth, it spins a silk thread with which it makes a house where it can rest. This house, made of silk threads, is called a cocoon.

Russell H. Anderson; Ewing Galloway

To get the silk, the cocoons are put in boiling water to make them soft. The silk thread is then unwound from the cocoon and put on big spools. It is now ready to be woven into cloth.

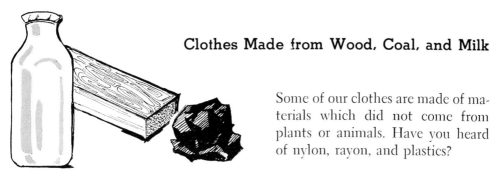

# Clothes Made from Wood, Coal, and Milk

Some of our clothes are made of materials which did not come from plants or animals. Have you heard of nylon, rayon, and plastics?

These three materials are made by mixing chemicals with air, water, and things which come from coal and wood.

This mixing of different materials makes liquids. These can be spun into threads by squeezing them through tiny holes. It is done by machines. They work somewhat the same as the silkworms do when they spin silk thread.

E. I. DuPont de Nemours & Co.

Which of the clothes shown on this page do you think were made from rayon? From nylon? From plastics? Ask your mother to show things in your home made from these materials.

## Clothes Made from Leather

The Indians and pioneers used animal skins for making many things. They used the skins of deer to make deerskin and buckskin. From these they made jackets, skirts, moccasins, and other useful things.

Today the skins of cows, horses, pigs, sharks, alligators, chamois, and snakes are used for making leather. From this leather we make jackets, shoes, gloves, handbags, belts, and other articles.

Armour Leather Co.

This is how leather is made. After the hair has been removed, the skins are put into a liquid made from the bark of trees. This liquid makes the skins tough, and keeps them from spoiling.

Then the skins are put into machines. The machines squeeze and rub the skins so that the leather will be soft. When this is done, it can be used to make many things.

## The Shoes We Wear

Most shoes are made from leather. A long time ago, shoes were made by hand. A man called a cobbler made them. Sometimes he traveled from one place to another to make shoes for grownups and for boys and girls.

Today, most shoes are made in factories by machines. This machine cuts the leather into the right size and shape.

Some of the machines make designs in the leather. Others put in the holes for the shoelaces.

Some of the machines sew the pieces of leather together. Other things needed for finishing the shoes are done by still other machines.

They can make high and low shoes. They can make shoes for work and for play. And they can make hundreds of shoes in one day.

## The Houses We Live in

Most people live in houses. These houses are not all the same, even in this country. Some are built of wood. Others are built of stone, brick, or metal. You may live in a house that stands alone. You may live in houses that are joined together. You may live in a big apartment building, high above the streets of your city. Or you may even live in a trailer, or mobile, home.

Ewing Galloway; H. Armstrong Roberts

The house you live in is your home. There you, your father and mother, and your brothers and sisters eat and sleep and play. There, too, you find shelter from cold, heat, rain, snow, wind, and other things from which you need protection.

**stone**

**wood**

Many materials are used to build a house. In pioneer days, houses were built of wood, of stone, or of sod. The pioneers used materials they found around them. Today, we have all kinds of other materials that we can use. Some of these come from faraway places.

Ewing Galloway

**metal**

**cement**

**glass**

**brick**

245

## Many Houses Are Made of Wood

One of the most important materials for building is wood. Some houses are almost entirely built of wood. Even homes built of brick and stone use wood on the inside. Wood is used for building walls and floors and roofs. It is also used for making furniture.

The wood we use comes from trees that grow in forests. The trees to be cut down are marked as shown.

By cutting a few trees only in this way, there will always be trees in the forest and there will be enough room for them to grow bigger and bigger.

Weyerhaeuser Timber Co., AFPI;
Standard Oil Co. of N. J.

Some of the logs are taken to the sawmill by trains and trucks.

Other logs are dumped into rivers. They are then floated to the sawmills.

In the sawmills, the logs are run through big machines, and cut into boards.

Then the boards are stacked and dried before they are taken to the lumber yard. There they are sold to the people who need them for building.

Here the wood that came from the forest is being used to build a house for some family.

## Other Houses
## Are Made of Brick and Stone

Not all houses are made of wood. Many are built of stone, especially when there is much of it near by. The stone is taken from places like this. They are called quarries.

Ewing Galloway: Brick and Clay Record

Other houses are built of bricks. The bricks are made from clay that is shaped, dried, and baked in special ovens.

248

## Houses Built of Man-Made Stone

Are you surprised to learn that we can make a stone which is often stronger and better than the stone we find around us? This man-made stone is called concrete.

Concrete is made by mixing one part of cement with two parts of sand and four parts of broken stone or gravel. Water is added, and the sand, cement, and gravel or broken stone are mixed together. It can be mixed by hand or by machine. At first it can be poured, but after a time it gets hard like solid rock.

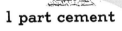

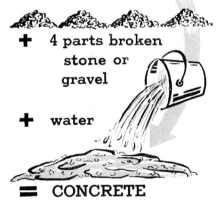

1 part cement

+ 2 parts sand

+ 4 parts broken stone or gravel

+ water

= CONCRETE

Portland Cement Assn.; Gregor, Monkmeyer; H. Armstrong Roberts

Here we see concrete being used to make the foundation of a house. This is the part of the house which is on or under the ground.

249

## Other Things Made of Concrete

Concrete is used for all kinds of things besides foundations for houses. Can you name some of the things shown on this page which are built of concrete?

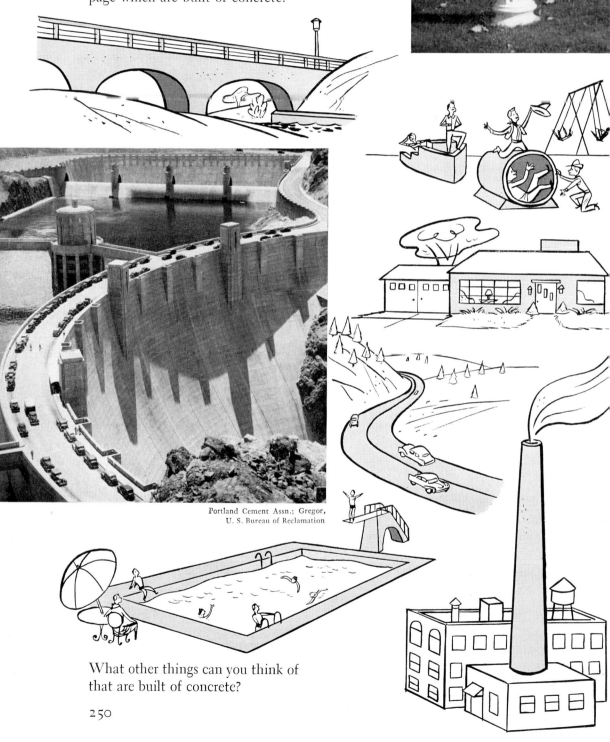

Portland Cement Assn.; Gregor,
U. S. Bureau of Reclamation

What other things can you think of that are built of concrete?

## Iron and Steel for Buildings

Iron and steel are used in building many homes, apartment buildings, offices, and factories. Steel is sometimes used to hold up the floors of our homes and make them strong. Iron and steel also are used sometimes for the frames or skeletons of apartment buildings.

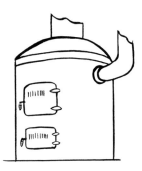

Iron and steel are used for making furnaces which heat our homes. They are also used in making

. . . the stoves on which we cook

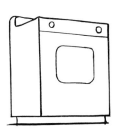

. . . the refrigerators which keep our food from spoiling

. . . washing machines, hot-water heaters, and other things.

What other articles made of iron and steel can you find in your home?

251

## Glass for Our Windows

Can you imagine living in a house which had no windows? Well, many boys and girls in pioneer days did. Even when there were windows, they did not always have glass in them. Instead, they were covered with animal skins.

As you look out of your windows at home, do you ever stop to think what glass is made of? It is hard to believe it is made mostly from sand. But it is.

First of all, sand is mixed in a big pot with limestone and other things. It is then cooked in a melting tank until the mixture melts.

Pittsburgh Plate Glass Co.; Ford Motor Co.

When the tank is emptied, out flows hot melted glass. Some of the glass is run between big rollers to make glass for windows in houses and cars.

252

## Other Objects Made of Glass

Sometimes, a glass blower picks up a gob of hot liquid glass on the end of a long hollow pipe. He blows air through the pipe and the glass blows up like a soap bubble. By blowing, swinging, and twisting, he can blow the glass into almost any shape he wants to. Machines are also used to shape glass into objects which we use. On this page, you will see many beautiful objects which have been made from glass.

Art Institute of Chicago

A bowl and tray from Sweden. The design shows a brilliant display of fireworks.

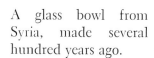

A glass bowl from Syria, made several hundred years ago.

Metropolitan
Museum of Art

A Steuben glass bowl with a graceful design.

Steuben Glass, U & U.

A solid crystal fish, made in an American glassworks.

Steuben Glass, U & U.

This glass mug, decorated with birds and flowers, was made in the United States more than 200 years ago.

Metropolitan Museum of Art

253

## Pots, Pans, and Dishes

What a funny place a home would be if there were no pots, pans, and dishes! But did you ever stop to think what they are made of? Some are made of clay which has been baked until it is hard. Others may be made of wood, iron, tin, copper, aluminum, or plastic.

This man is making a plate from moist clay. He is shaping the plate with the piece of wood he is holding in his left hand.

Some dishes are made in molds like this.

Lenox, Inc.

Pots and pans like these are usually made of metal.

## Other Objects Made of Clay

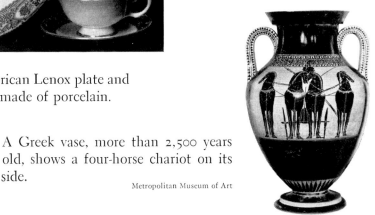

Lenox, Inc.

Since the earliest times, people have made beautiful objects from clay. Some of these are shown on this page.

This beautiful American Lenox plate and cup and saucer are made of porcelain.

A Greek vase, more than 2,500 years old, shows a four-horse chariot on its side.

Metropolitan Museum of Art

The Chinese made this pottery horse with saddle blankets nearly 2,000 years ago.

Art Institute of Chicago

This small statue of a Javanese girl was made in Denmark.

Metropolitan Museum of Art

An Indian jar from Mexico. Look carefully, and you will see that the design on it is a face.

Buffalo Museum of Science

255

## How a House Is Built

Before any house can be built, some-one has to plan what it is to look like and how it is to be built. That person is called an architect. Here he is showing his plans to a father and mother.

They told him what kind of house they wanted. They told him how big it was to be—how many rooms it was to have—what kind of rooms—and how they were to be arranged. They also told him whether they wanted it of wood, stone, or brick.

They wanted a basement. So a hole was dug in the ground by a digging machine. A wood mold was built against the sides of the hole. Concrete was then poured into the mold. This was the foundation upon which the house was built.

Trenches were dug in the ground for the water pipes and gas pipes, and for the pipes to carry away the waste water.

Ewing Galloway; Harold Lambert

Carpenters built the framework. This frame was then cov-ered with boards.

Men put on a roof of wooden shingles. Sometimes asbestos, slate, or tile is used.

Men called plumbers put in the pipes for the water used in the basement, kitchen, and bathroom. They also put in the gas pipes.

Other men, called electricians, put in the wires, fuse boxes, switches, wall plugs, and lights.

Still other men put in the furnace.

The floors were then laid by the carpenters. They also finished all the inside woodwork, and put in the windows.

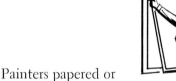

Ewing Galloway; Harold Lambert; H. Armstrong Roberts

Painters papered or painted the walls.

The house is now ready for the family to move in their furniture and other things they need.

257

## How Houses Are Heated

In countries where the winters are cold, houses must be heated.

Some houses have fireplaces where logs can be burned. Many years ago, this was the only way to heat houses.

Ewing Galloway

Furnaces are usually put in the basement. They use coal, gas, or oil. Some homes are heated by electricity.

Some furnaces heat the air which is carried through pipes to various parts of the house.

Other furnaces heat water that is carried through pipes to radiators. These are set up in each room.

In some houses, pipes under the floor, in the ceiling, or behind the baseboards carry hot water to keep the house warm.

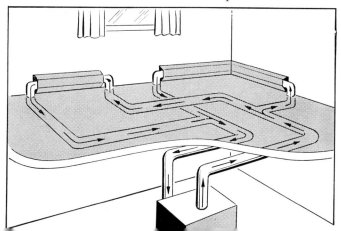

## How We Travel

Long ago, in pioneer and colonial days, people had to travel on foot and on horseback. They traveled in stagecoaches or in covered wagons.

Because the roads were poor, it was easier to travel along the rivers and lakes. People went by canoe, by raft, and later by horse-drawn boats and steamboats.

Today, we can travel by car or by bus over wonderful roads. We can go by train or by ship. And we can fly in fast airplanes across land or sea. You can fly across the country in one day. You can have breakfast in New York, lunch in Chicago, and be in San Francisco in time for dinner.

Ewing Galloway; Pa. Turnpike Commission; Greyhound; New York Central System; TWA

259

## Cars, Buses, and Trucks

Perhaps more people travel by car than in any other way. We use cars to go to the store, to the post office and other places, and in making long trips.

Many people travel by bus. The bus is really a car, too, but it has been made large enough to carry more people.

Still other people travel in small and large trucks. In this way, they can carry things with them as they travel.

Division of Highways, California; Greyhound; Fruehauf; GMC Truck & Coach Division

From what are these cars and buses and trucks made? Some of the things needed in building them are rubber, steel, glass, copper, nickel, chromium, plastics, cotton, and wood. What other things can you think of?

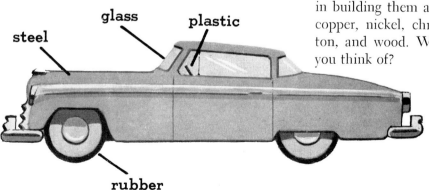

steel    glass    plastic

rubber

## What Makes a Car Go?

A car will not go without gasoline to make the engine go. It must have oil to make the gears turn smoothly. It must have water in the radiator to keep the engine from getting too hot. And it must have enough air in the tires so that people who use the car can ride in it quite comfortably.

Pure Oil Co.

This car is getting gas at the filling station. The man has checked the oil, water, and tires. He is now filling the gas tank.

The engine makes the back wheels turn so the car can go.

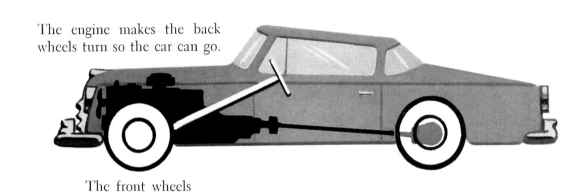

The front wheels are used to steer.

The battery starts the engine. It can also run the lights, the radio, the horn, and the heater when the engine is not running. When the engine runs, it turns a small generator which produces electricity to make these things work.

horn

lights

radio

starter

heater

261

## Where Does the Gasoline Come From?

Where did the filling-station man get the gasoline he puts in your car?

Gasoline is made from oil which is found deep under ground.

This oil is pumped to the surface and stored in large tanks like this.

Then it is pumped through big pipes to a big place, where it is made into gasoline and oil for your car. Some of it also is made into oil for your furnace, and into other products.

Trucks bring the gasoline to the filling station.

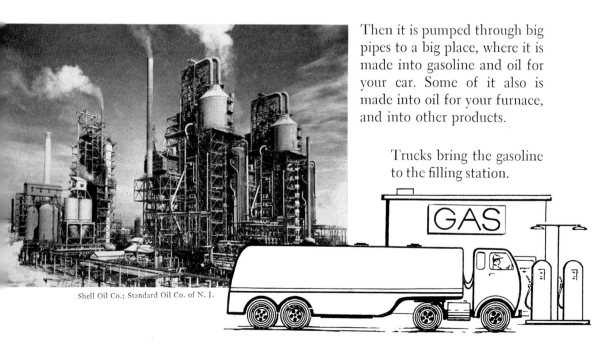

Shell Oil Co.; Standard Oil Co. of N. J.

262

## Rubber Tires to Ride on

Rubber is made from a sticky juice called latex. It runs out of cuts that are made in the bark of rubber trees like these. Pure rubber is made from the latex by adding chemicals or by letting it dry out. The rubber is then rolled into sheets and hung up to dry.

This man is building up a tire on a tire-making machine. First, he puts on several layers of cloth. Then he adds a material made of cord which protects the tire from the rim. These layers are next covered with rubber to form a flat-shaped tire.

Ewing Galloway; Goodyear Tire & Rubber Co.

The flat-shaped tire is then put in this molding machine. It is heated and blown into shape. Out of the mold comes a tire shaped like this.

263

This is a small, two-passenger plane.

## We Fly Through the Air

You can travel fast in a car or bus, but you can go even faster in a plane.

This airplane with four engines is used to carry people great distances. It will fly across continents and over the oceans. When a plane has several engines, it can still fly, even if one or two engines stop working.

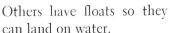

Others have floats so they can land on water.

Some airplanes have skis instead of wheels so they can land on ice and snow.

Still other airplanes have special engines called jets. They need no propellers.

Ryan Aeronautical Co.; Eastern Air Lines; Cessna Aircraft Co.; Lockheed Aircraft Corp.; Bell Aircraft Corp.

This airplane has no wings, but it can fly up, down, sideways, forward, and backward. It is a helicopter.

264

## Over the Rails We Go!

This engine runs by steam.

How exciting it is to take a trip on a train! There are two kinds of trains—trains for carrying goods and trains for carrying people. Freight trains, like the one at the bottom of the page, carry goods. Passenger trains, like the one at the top of the page, carry people and mail.

All trains must have engines. These are not all the same.

This one is run by electricity.

Southern Pacific Lines; Union Pacific Railroad; Pennsylvania Railroad; Great Northern Railway; H. Armstrong Roberts

This one uses oil.

If you go a long way on the train, you can eat and sleep on it, too. This is the dining car where you eat your meals.

And you would sleep in a bed like this.

Some railroads are built just for fun.

## Over Bridges and
## Under Mountains and Rivers

Just imagine what it was like before bridges and tunnels were built! In crossing our country, the pioneers found it hard to cross the big rivers. They also found it hard to travel with their wagons over land that had many mountains.

Today, we find it easy to travel over high and low places by car, bus, or train. We can do this because bridges have been built across the rivers and low places.

Tunnels have also been built through many mountains.

Oregon State Highway Commission;
Union Pacific Railroad;
Chicago Transit Authority;
Port of New York Authority

Sometimes, entire railroads are built underground. Such railroads are called subways.

This shows the inside of a tunnel that goes under the wide Hudson River. It links New York City with Jersey City.

## Across Rivers, Lakes, and Oceans

Just as we have two kinds of trains, so, too, we have two kinds of ships—ships for carrying goods and ships for carrying people.

Big ships such as this one carry people across the ocean.

This ferryboat also carries people across rivers and bays. It goes back and forth, back and forth.

These boats are used mostly for fun.

Fairchild Aerial Surveys; Oregon State Highway Commission; U. S. Bureau of Reclamation; Harold Lambert; Suzanne Szasz

This lake boat is carrying iron ore to the steel mills.

A tanker is used to carry oil and gasoline across the ocean. Why do you suppose it is called a tanker?

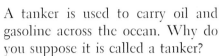

A tow boat on the Ohio River pushes a string of twelve loaded barges ahead of it.

Ewing Galloway

Sometimes freight trains bring goods right to the water's edge. There the goods are put on the ships which take them to faraway lands. Goods brought by the ships from faraway lands also are put on the trains which carry them to the places where they are to be used.

## Coal for Steam and Heat

Many of the engines that pull our trains still use coal to make the steam which makes them go. And so do many ships. Many houses and other buildings also are heated by coal furnaces. Where does the coal come from? Sometimes we find it near the surface, and sometimes we find it deep down under the ground.

These two miners are deep underground in a coal mine. They are drilling a hole in a wall of coal.

Pickow, Three Lions

Another man is putting dynamite in the holes. When the dynamite is exploded, it breaks the coal into many pieces.

The coal is then loaded into a small car by this machine.

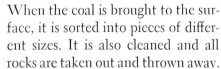

When the coal is brought to the surface, it is sorted into pieces of different sizes. It is also cleaned and all rocks are taken out and thrown away.

Then the coal is loaded on big cars and taken where it is to be used.

# How We Share What We Know

### Talking

person to person

by telephone

recording machines

How things have changed! A hundred years ago there were no telephones, no radios, and no television sets. Even books and newspapers were scarce.

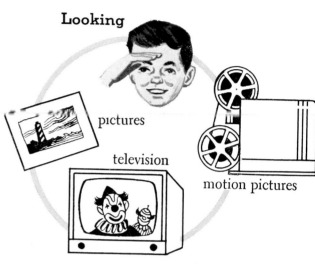

### Looking

pictures

television

motion pictures

Today, things are different. Because of the telephone, radio, and television, we know almost immediately what is going on in the world. Men of science and men of business and industry have given us many helps for talking, looking, listening, writing, and reading . . . helps for sharing with others what we think and know.

### Listening

speaking

radio

records

### Writing

by hand

shorthand

typewriter

### Reading

books

letters

magazines

newspapers

# Where Does Your Telephone Reach?

Your telephone at home can help you reach many places with your voice. You can talk to people in other parts of your town, state, or country. You can even talk with people who live across the sea.

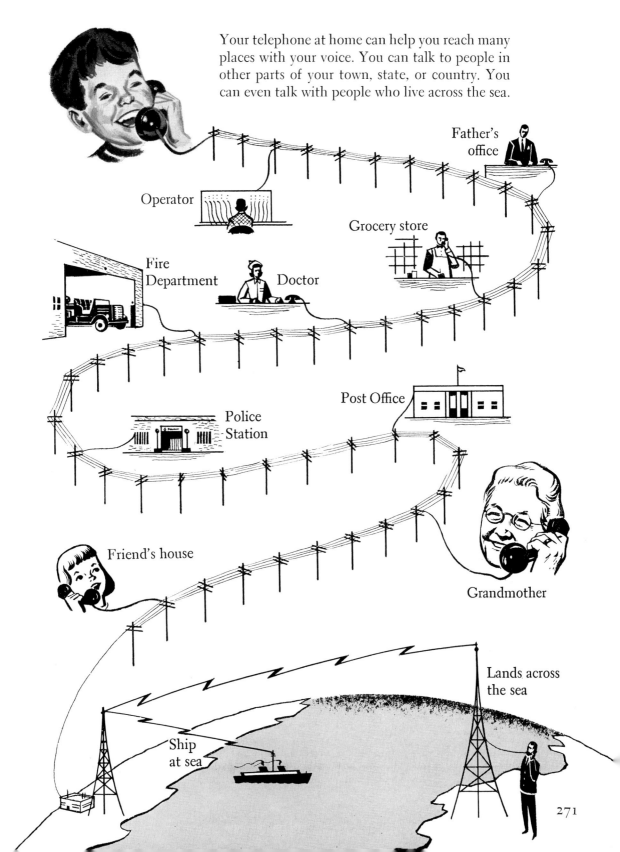

Father's office

Operator

Grocery store

Fire Department

Doctor

Police Station

Post Office

Grandmother

Friend's house

Lands across the sea

Ship at sea

271

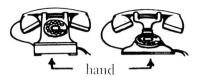

## How to Use the Telephone

hand

wall

stand

coin

There are many kinds of telephones. Some have dials and some do not. But every telephone has a mouthpiece and a receiver.

When you use the telephone, hold the receiver close to your ear. Speak directly into the mouthpiece—this way . . .

not like this

. . . or like this

Hibbs

If you do not have a dial telephone, be sure to tell the operator, in a clear voice, the number you want.

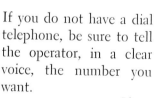

If you do have a dial phone, you will need to dial the number carefully so you will get it right. There are several kinds of dials, but they all work the same way.

When the telephone rings at the other end, wait about a minute for the person to answer before you decide he is not there.

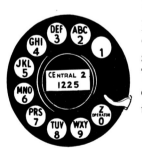

When you use the telephone, always be polite. Even if the person you are talking to cannot see you, he can tell what sort of person you are from the way you speak.

Oh, that's all right.

I am so sorry. I have the wrong number.

Be pleasant if someone calls your number by mistake.

Apologize if you should call or get the wrong number.

Dad is out in the garage. He will be right in.

If it takes a little time for someone called to come to the telephone, go back to the telephone and explain.

O. K., Uncle Joe. I'll tell mother as soon as she gets home.

If the person called is not home, offer to take the message or ask for the caller's number so he or she can be called back.

We'd better stop now—someone else may want to use the line.

Don't be selfish if you are on a party line. Share the telephone with others.

## Listening to Radio

What a difference radio has made in the way we live! Without leaving our homes, we can listen to music, to sports broadcasts, and to other programs. Radio helps us all. It helps the police, airmen, and others in the work they have to do. It warns us when bad weather is on the way. It tells the farmer what prices he can get for the animals and crops he has to sell.

This is a play which is being sent out over the radio. You will notice that the actor is speaking into a microphone. This picks up the voices and other sounds that are made.

Sound effects on a radio program are made in different ways.

CBS; NBC

These voices and sounds are sent over wires by electricity to this big tower. It is a transmitter. It sends out radio waves of the voices and sounds, in all directions.

The children are listening to a radio program. The radio waves sent out by the transmitter are caught by the radio receiver in the home. There, they are changed back into voices and sounds.

274

NBC

## Looking at Television

Radio makes it possible for you to listen. Television makes it possible for you to see as well as to hear. Television pictures are sent out through the air in about the same way that radio sounds are sent out. Here are a few of the things that happen.

A television camera like this is used to show what is happening.

It may be photographing a puppet show.

As the camera photographs what is happening, sight and sound signals go by wire to the transmitter. There, the signals are sent out in all directions.

H. Armstrong Roberts

The home receiver picks up the sight and sound signals by means of an antenna and changes the signals back to picture and sound.

These boys and girls are enjoying a television program.

## Books to Read and Enjoy

Long ago, the only books were those which were written by hand. Mostly, this work was done by the monks.

When the Pilgrims landed at Plymouth Rock, the only books they had were those they brought with them. Mostly, they were hymn books, Bibles, and books written about the Bible.

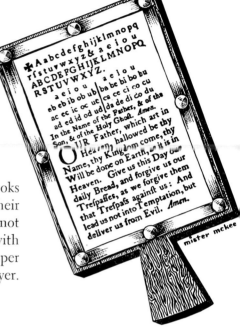

mister mckee

The children of the Pilgrims had no books written especially for them. One of their first books was the Hornbook, which was not really a book at all. It was a flat board with a handle. On it was pasted a piece of paper showing the alphabet and the Lord's Prayer.

Things are different now, for we have books for everyone. There are books for young and old, and there are books on almost every subject.

McKee, Public Service Bulletin;
Kroch's & Brentano's; Kingsport Press

Most books are now made by machines which can print many thousands of pages in a day. The pages are put together and covers are then put on. Here is a machine putting covers on CHILD-CRAFT.

# Books
# for Everything

You can enjoy picture books

or comic books.

You can buy
spelling books
and readers

and
encyclopedias.

There are also map books

and books on how to make things.

## Where Books Are Kept

There is a kind of magic in books. In imagination, they can take you deep into the earth or down below the surface of the sea. They can take you into the jungle, to the top of the highest mountains, or across the hot desert. They can even take you in a rocket ship to the moon.

Besides CHILDCRAFT, you will have other books in your home. And if you don't have what you want at home, you can go to the library. There you will find

. . . books to take out

. . . magazines to read

. . . music to listen to

H. Armstrong Roberts

. . . and pictures to look at.

278

## Reading the Newspaper

A newspaper tells us in words and pictures what is going on in the world. Some newspapers are printed every day. Others are printed every week or every month. How are they prepared?

First the news must be gathered by men called reporters. This is sent in to the newspaper offices by telephone, by telegraph, by radio, and in many other ways. The news stories are then written and prepared for printing.

Pictures of people and happenings are taken by photographers. These, too, are prepared for printing.

Ewing Galloway; Chicago Tribune; H. Armstrong Roberts

Here is a printing press which does the printing. The paper goes in at one end. The news and pictures are printed on it. The paper is cut and folded and comes out at the other end as newspapers.

It takes only a few hours from the time the news happens until it is printed and the paper is delivered to your home.

## Learning from Pictures

Sometimes we learn as much from pictures as we do from words. Through pictures of all kinds we share our knowledge with others.

Such pictures may be photographs, film strips, comic strips, drawings, cartoons, maps, or motion pictures. They may be black and white pictures or they may be printed in beautiful colors, as many of them are shown in CHILDCRAFT. Just imagine living in a world which had no pictures! Reading and learning would be much slower and not half as much fun.

A good photograph like this helps us to know what a waterfall is like.

This picture helps those who live far from the sea know what the shore looks like.

Gendreau; Hibbs;

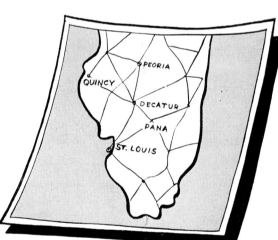

A map tells us where to find places and how to get there.

© 1954, Walt Kelly

An animal cartoon is something which pleases everybody.

Is there anyone who has not laughed at a funny comic strip?

A picture such as this always gives us pleasure when we look at it.

A series of film-strip pictures can show us what is happening, step by step.

Rules are necessary when we go traveling on the highways....

....on the railroads....

...on the high seas....

....in the air....

...and even when we ride bicycles.

Ewing Galloway; H. Armstrong Roberts; Popular Science Publishing Co.; Bell & Howell Co.

Motion pictures also help to teach us and to give us enjoyment.

## The Paper We Use

Not a day goes by but that you see and use paper. Where does it come from? How is it made? Perhaps you will be surprised to learn that most of our paper is made from wood. The best paper of all is made from rags.

Logs like these are put in a machine which removes the bark.

The logs are then washed and cut into chips. These are put in big tanks where they are cooked to make wood pulp.

West Virginia Pulp & Paper Co.; Weyerhauser Timber Co.

The wood pulp is made white, washed, and then put in a paper-making machine like this. There it is pressed thin and flat and comes out as paper.

## Some Things for Which Paper Is Used

Think of all the things for which paper is used. Some of them are shown here. What other things made of paper can you think of?

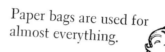

We couldn't make books, magazines, or newspapers without paper.

Stores use paper for wrapping.

Paper bags are used for almost everything.

And so are cartons.

H. Armstrong Roberts

We use paper tissues to blow our noses.

Playing cards are made from paper.

Stamps, too, are made of paper.

Blotting paper and paper towels are things we use.

And just suppose there were no writing paper!

283

# Other Ways in Which Science and Industry Help Us

### Fighting Fires

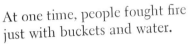

Long ago, man found out how to make fire. He found it to be very useful. But if he was careless, he also found it dangerous and harmful. That is why we must not play with matches, fireworks, and fire.

At one time, people fought fire just with buckets and water.

Today, fire alarms can be sent in quickly from electric boxes.

Hook and ladder trucks dash to the fire.

Hoses are connected with the water hydrant.

The pumper engine forces water through hoses at high pressure.

Sometimes fires in the home put out by small extinguish which are filled with chemical

## Helping Our Policemen to Help Us

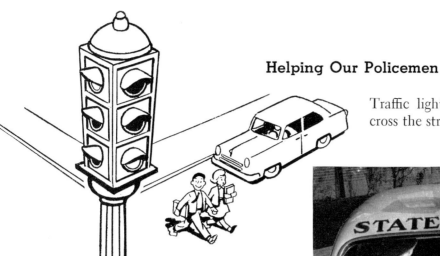

Traffic lights help us to cross the streets safely.

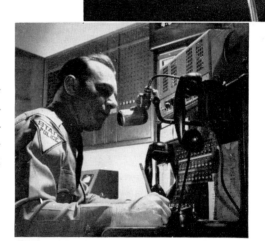

Motor bicycles and cars help our police friends move around faster than if they were walking.

With the help of radio, they can keep in touch with the police station and with other police cars when they are protecting us from those who break the law.

Fingerprinting helps them to find out who the lawbreakers are.

Big cities even have their own laboratories where science helps to protect innocent people and to find the guilty ones.

## Helping to Keep Us Well

The doctor has all kinds of instruments to help him find out whether people are ill, and to help make them well.

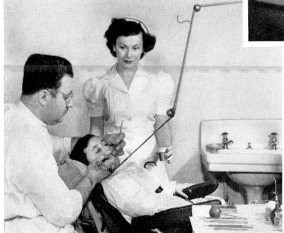

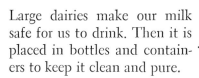

The dentist, too, has instruments to help him keep our teeth strong and healthy.

Large dairies make our milk safe for us to drink. Then it is placed in bottles and containers to keep it clean and pure.

Garbage trucks have been built to take away rubbish and waste.

The water we drink is made pure before it is pumped into our homes.

Ambulances take sick people to the hospital. There the finest equipment is ready to help make them well again.

286

## Making it Easier for Us to Learn

When we go to school, men of science and men in business have made all kinds of products that will help us learn more easily, more comfortably, and more quickly.

The desks you sit in were made for your comfort.

Equipment in the gymnasium and playground help to keep you strong and healthy.

Maps and globes help you learn about the world.

American Seating Co.; H. Armstrong Roberts

The science classroom has all kinds of things to help you understand and learn.

# Looking Ahead

Men in science and in industry are always looking ahead. They want to find better ways of doing things. They ask, "What will it be like when the boys and girls of today grow up?"

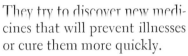

They try to discover new medicines that will prevent illnesses or cure them more quickly.

They are working toward better, faster, and safer ways of traveling.

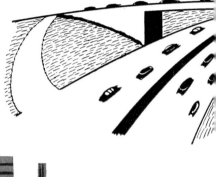

They are planning cities where everyone can live in comfort.

They want to use power from the atom and from the sun to work for us.

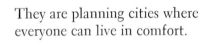

Some of you will grow up to work in science. Others will be working in business and in industry. Together, science and industry will work even greater wonders by the time you are grown up.

288